THE

GRAND

DESIGN

volume 1

THE

GRAND

DESIGN

volume 1

A SIMPLY STATED, USER-FRIENDLY
GUIDE TO LIVING IN THE UNIVERSE

PADDY MCMAHON

HAMPTON ROADS
PUBLISHING COMPANY, INC.

Cover design by Marjoram Productions
Cover painting by Nick Gonzalez

For information write:
Hampton Roads Publishing Company, Inc.
1125 Stoney Ridge Rd.
Charlottesville, VA 22902
Or call: 804-296-2772
FAX: 804-296-5096
e-mail: hrpc@hrpub.com
Web site: www.hrpub.com

If you are unable to order this book from your local
bookseller, you may order directly from the publisher.
Quantity discounts for organizations are available.
Call 1-800-766-8009, toll-free.

Library of Congress Catalog Card Number: 99-95404
ISBN 1-57174-154-2

10 9 8 7 6 5 4 3 2 1

Printed on acid-free paper in Canada

Table of Contents

PART III

PART IV

PART V

PART VI

Introduction by Paddy McMahon

In my earlier life I never envisaged myself doing this sort of writing. I was always very interested in writing and tended to find myself in positions, in terms of career, where I had to do a lot of writing. I wanted more than that though. Above all, I wanted to be a famous playwright; not just a playwright, but a famous one!

I was born in July 1933, in a rather remote part of County Clare, in Ireland. Stories of ghosts and fairies and the banshee, a female spirit who always seemed to be combing her hair and in attitudes of mourning, were very much part of my childhood. There were fairy forts and pathways and bushes which were "out of bounds" for playing in, or walking on, or touching, or using in any way. All this was taken seriously by young and old alike, but mixed with orthodox Roman Catholicism in a curious blend of wonder dominated and limited by fear.

My mother was deeply religious and observant of all the rules and regulations to the best of her abilities. My father wasn't, and in fact, gave up the practice of religion altogether when I was still very young. Images of a patriarchal, judgmental God and of eternal punishment through the indescribable tortures of hell were given a more personal reality for me because of my constant fear that my father, whom I loved very much, would die without having had a chance to repent of his sins.

When I was thirteen I went to boarding school where there was a heavy emphasis on religion and the desirability of becoming priests. There were times when the theatricality of being a priest appealed to me; the special clothes, the aura of mystery and of power, captive audiences, being called "Father" and treated with great respect. Really, though, I never had any intention of becoming a priest, in spite of the fact that I was very religious during my teens. While there was an ever-present consciousness of the supernatural or the paranormal, there was a lot of fear associated with it; fear of punishment, hell, devils, spirits generally, and, in particular, evil spirits. I can't remember anything particularly unusual about myself in a psychic context. I never saw any spirits, not even the banshee!

The one thing out of the ordinary that stands out in my memory happened when I was nineteen years old. In 1952 I had a job in the Civil Service in Dublin. I went home to County Clare for the Christmas holidays. When I was leaving home to go back to Dublin, my father went with me to the bus station. As he was saying goodbye to me I knew with an inner certainty that I wouldn't see him alive again, and I knew he knew. I resolved that I would write him a long letter saying all the things that I had never been able to say to him, at least, not since I was a child. But I hadn't done so by the time I got a telephone call late in February 1953, to tell me that he had died suddenly after a brief illness.

There was no obvious deathbed repentance as far as my father was concerned. I didn't want to believe, nor did I believe, that he could end up in a place of eternal punishment. In any case, I think I had begun to move away at that stage from the orthodox belief structure that I had grown up with. If anything, my feelings surrounding my father's death accelerated that process rather than initiated it. From an early age I'd been a voracious, if not a discriminating reader and in my late teens and through my twenties and early thirties I was deeply interested and involved in theater activities and did a lot of amateur acting and direction. I practiced and enjoyed all of these activities in and for themselves, but my goal was also to gain experience to fulfill my ultimate aim of being a famous playwright. The exposure to a wide variety of ideas through reading, and my experience in the theater, clearly contributed to an open mind able to think beyond the rather narrow confines of my own conditioning.

I got married, had two children, and progressed in my career as a civil servant. My life fitted into fairly predictable routines, and I dabbled with writing plays, all the while telling myself that I would make a real go of it when I could retire from the Civil Service at age sixty. I managed to write a few plays and entered them into occasional competitions and sent them to some theater managements without success, with the exception of one competition where my entry was considered meritorious enough to allow me to be considered for inclusion in a panel of television writers. That, too, I put on the long finger waiting for the perceived paradise of retirement.

Then in my early forties a new world opened up for me, which, as it evolved, made my ambition to become a playwright, even a famous one, fade into the background and lose all its significance for me. Until I came to write this I had forgotten that a trigger point for me was seeing a book in a public library entitled, *A World Beyond*, by Ruth Montgomery. I borrowed the book and was fascinated by the scenario of life after death which it presented through communication received by Ruth Montgomery from Arthur Ford, who was well known as a medium during his Earth life, from which he departed in 1971. Shortly after reading that book I heard about guides, which really turned life around, upside down, and downside up, for me.

I grew up with a strong belief in guardian angels. I found it a wonderfully comforting thing as a child. I used to talk to them then, but I don't remember ever having heard them talking back to me; just as well, probably, or I'd have been terrified, given the exposure to ghosts I was experiencing. But I thought of my guardian angels as my friends and there was no fear associated with them as long as I couldn't see them or hear them. Later on after my father died, I was terrified of seeing him, much as I loved him when he was in his physical body; such is the influence of conditioning.

At the age of forty-four, early in 1978, I began to see and hear angels; a matter of fact statement which covers a plethora of mixed emotions. I was thrilled, intrigued, delighted, and, at the same time, disturbed. All the doubts and fears of my conditioning came to the surface. Was it "good" or "bad"? Was I imagining it all? Was it the devil and all his cohorts of evil spirits playing tricks on me? Was I simply going mad? Walking along streets with people (in physical bodies) all around me, I could hear other conversations in the air. Sitting in trains, I got visions of other civilizations and other ages. I looked at people sitting near me, chatting, reading newspapers or books, gazing out the windows, or just sitting silently, and I wondered about reality. Could they see any of what I was seeing? It didn't seem so. Were they the lucky ones to be unconscious of it all? Would I be better off if I could go back to being the way I was? I didn't want to be back there, but I found it very difficult to cope with ordinary everyday life. I wanted to get away by myself to savor it all, and yet I felt I had to continue with my daily routines as if nothing was happening. I was distracted and difficult to live with. Yet, strangely, people I worked with didn't seem to notice anything unusual about me.

After a few months I realized that I couldn't go on living in what seemed like a multiplicity of worlds. Since I was on planet Earth, I'd either have to leave it or be grounded in the experience of it. Then it came to me that the answer was simple: I could just ask my guides to control what was coming to me, to let it happen only by arrangement. I asked and, miraculously, my life returned to "normal," or sort of normal. Perversely, I missed the excitement and wonder of all the continuing communication, but at least I was able to function within the physical reality of my environment.

Now, though life, externally, had settled back into some kind of normality, the internal change was enormous. Life had opened up into a vista of never-ending, evolving conscious-ness, which put all the happenings of day-to-day existence into a totally new perspective. And yet it wasn't new. Somewhere deep inside me I had known it all the time, and the unfolding process, as I began to write down what was coming to me, became a joyful and wonderful journeying to the surface of my awareness. The name "Shebaka" didn't mean anything to me other than that I liked the sound of it, which I found easy to accept. At the time I think I'd have found it very hard to accept a name that had historical associations for me. As it was, no preconceptions intruded on my consciousness.

The writing of these books with Shebaka was not, in any sense, automatic. I was aware of Shebaka, but not in a visu-al or obvious way. It's hard to explain; I could feel a presence and powerful energy flowing through me. Yet the energy was gentle and totally non-directive. I wrote in my own way and my own time and within the capacity of my own vocabulary and my own style. Ideas, concepts, facts were presented to me in a broad, yet unmistakable, way. I had to think a lot about some of them before I could put words on them, and sometimes I felt it very difficult to express accurately in words what was emerging into my consciousness. More and more I was being faced with the limitations of words and I can now see more clearly why complete, unambiguous com-munication is virtually impossible to achieve verbally. Yet we have to deal in words within the restrictions of our Earth existence, so it is in our interest to do the best we can.

The title, *The Grand Design,* suggested itself and it encapsulates what the material is about. Essentially, it aims to celebrate the existence of an infinite, all-comprehending, cooperative chain of love linking all souls together, yet with total respect for their individuality and free will. This in a re-learning, often painful, process of reaching back into a fullness of awareness lost so long ago by a small proportion, but a vast number, of all the souls in the universe.

The existence and availability of guides (guardian angels) to all of us is a central theme. My childhood concept of guardian angels was of beings with wings under which I could shelter and let go of all my troubles. My present concept is fundamentally not much different except that I understand how guides have evolved to be what they are and, of course, the wings are symbolic rather than real. My initial communication with guides was very obvious; as obvious, although not in terms of sound, as somebody talking to me. Then, as time went on, it became less and less obvious, so that I wondered whether it was all gone away, which left me feeling desolate and abandoned. But after a while, I realized that I was being guided to see the communication as an integral part of myself rather than as something external to me. I am not an automaton or a robot but, rather, an essential player, as everybody is, in the whole process of life, and part of my purpose in life is to show that there is no mystery about communication. It is something that fits into people's lives in the most natural possible ways without even having to think about it. I came to understand that what guides are aiming to achieve is to help us reach more and more of the fullness of our own potential without, at the same time, interfering with our free will, so that we always retain control of our own choices. It follows, then, that guidance has to be unobtrusive and non-directive and is generally designed to help us find and benefit from opportunities for growth in line with our life purpose.

While I had been communicating regularly with other guides since 1978, I didn't have my first conscious communication with Shebaka until 1981. The sessions recorded in these books ranged over the following fifteen years. During that time, I continued to experience Shebaka as a presence, rather than in any familiarly identifiable way, such as male or female, or appearance. It didn't even occur to me to attempt such identification, as it didn't seem appropriate since "he" had moved beyond identification in that way.

In 1996, I met a man who asked me if I knew that there was a Shebaka stone in the British Museum in London. That was the first I had heard of it. I read later that the stone is called after a King Shabaka, who reigned in Egypt from 712 to 698 BC. On one of his expeditions, he discovered a scroll on which the story of creation, according to the god Ptah, was recorded. The scroll had been partially destroyed by worms. He arranged that the surviving part of it should be carved in stone in order to preserve it; hence the name of the stone. Unfortunately, the stone was later used for milling purposes and some of the inscriptions at its center were obliterated.

During the session entitled "Dialogue with Shebaka" at the end of the second volume, Shebaka confirmed that that was one of his male incarnations. That was an extraordinarily affirming development for me, particularly coming, as it did, at the end of our fifteen year collaboration, rather than at the beginning. It was as if time stood still. Some two thousand seven hundred years ago, Shebaka considered the material in the scrolls so important that he sought to preserve what was left of it for posterity in the best way he knew. He was only partially successful. That doesn't matter now. Through his expanded awareness, the story of creation, and much more besides, is recorded and preserved in a different way. The past has been subsumed into the present and transformed.

Because I didn't know in 1981 that there had been such a person as Shebaka, I had no guideline in spelling the name. I went along with my own impression of it and used "e" in the first syllable, whereas in the British Museum version "a" is used—Shab instead of Sheb. I'll stay with my own version. He doesn't care what spelling is used; he has long since transcended that incarnation.

While there's an underlying interlinking philosophy running through all the sessions in the books, the aim is that, for easy reading, each session is as accessible as possible on its own, without a lot of reference to earlier material. This necessarily involves some repetition; although the primary objective of whatever repetition there is in some of the sessions is reinforcement of the basic teachings in the communications as a whole.

Even though our "formal" communication ceased in 1996, Shebaka has not abandoned me. In fact, as I'm writing this, I'm receiving a clear message from him, in which I want to join. It is one of profound gratitude to all the wonderful people in the Hampton Roads Publishing Company who are involved in the publication of the books, in particular, Pat Adler, for her sensitively accomplished and empathic editing, and the Art Department, for the beautifully designed covers. Special thanks, also, to Marianne, our agent, for her unfailing enthusiasm and heartfelt dedication; to Jim, for having so helpfully provided the key to the door, so to speak; and to Maura, for her unstinting, loving encouragement, and her flair for finding solutions rather than humoring problems.

In the early stages of my communication with guides, the constant feeling of humor and joy coming from them intrigued me. That seemed to be totally at odds with the concept of spirituality of my conditioning which didn't seem to have much joy in it. Indeed, a feeling of joy would have been a source of guilt, given that self-denial and penance paved the way to heaven. So, after some time, I asked my guides how was it that there was always such a feeling of joy coming from them. The answer that came through to me in a humorously direct way was, "So you want us to be miserable?" And then it was explained to me that the essence of spirituality is joy; that the more true we are to ourselves, the more we express joy; and in being more truly ourselves, the more centered we are in our own energy, and the more we can help others. If we're miserable, we only spread misery.

Finally, I hope that any readers who have manifested themselves in female form in their present incarnations won't be offended by my use of "he" where "he/she" would be appropriate, but too cumbersome for easy reading. Thanks for your understanding.

Paddy McMahon
November 1999

Introduction by Shebaka

At last I am come to send you greetings and to hope that we will have long and happy association. I impress my thoughts on your mind and you are converting them into your words. I will go slowly so that you will have time to put in your beloved punctuation marks!

I have let myself be called Shebaka because I know the sound of the name would have a certain appeal to you but in reality I have no name. I am coming to talk to you from a vibration where names are no longer important, where indeed communication is instantaneous and is so open that one communicates simply by being. Thus there is never any misunderstanding. I retain a memory of the circumstances of Earth and I know the constraints they put on communication.

Why am I especially coming to communicate through you? Because this is part of our purpose, that you would develop yourself to the stage where it would be possible for me to relay to you some of the wisdom to which it is my privilege to have access. You in turn will find opportunities to pass on this distilled wisdom to others who may be interested.

I am no stuffy higher being, I just happen to be in a higher vibration. Nor do I want to set myself up as a know-all, nor as an object of veneration, nor as a symbol of sanctity. I only tell you about the higher vibration to reassure you, and anybody else who might have access to these words, that I speak with some authority, having progressed through many stages of evolutionary growth. I will be talking about these stages later, but if you want to think in terms of seven then I come at present from the sixth stage. I am also in a position to describe the seventh stage.

All of what I might call your spiritual reading has been nudged in a certain direction and I have been in the background keeping a "hooded eye" over the communications that have already come to you. I only mention this for reassurance.

It is not necessary to make an appointment for certain times to do this writing unless you want to do that. For me time does not exist in your terms, so it is up to you. I await your invitation whenever and wherever suits you. I can tune into your thoughts at any time and you are finding that you have no difficulty in tuning into mine.

If I don't use any form of salutation or greeting it is not that I don't wish to convey good wishes but that I want to convey the continuity of my contact. So you can take that for granted.

You wish that our communication be more obvious, maybe that I would show myself and sit opposite you while we're talking. It's not possible for me to do that at this stage. I am too far removed from the Earth vibration to be able to assume its physical characteristics without a lot of preparation. So you'll have to take me on trust.

PART I

Light Is the Illumination of the Soul

Today I would like very briefly to discuss the significance of light. You know it within its ordinary meaning as something by which you see, such as the light of day, or electric light, or even the light of understanding. There is of course also light meaning not heavy. But light in a spiritual sense means much more. It is illumination of the soul, of the whole being, so that ultimately all darkness is gone. Light spreads and eliminates (not illuminates, although that may come first) darkness. This is also tied in with vibration. The Earth is a heavy vibration and so is the physical body that keeps the soul chained to that heaviness. At physical death the soul (or real being) leaves the heaviness behind and is no longer constrained by the limitations of that heaviness. It is feeling light as opposed to heavy although it has probably not yet eliminated the darkness of misunderstanding from its perceptions. It is a strange paradox that the assumption of heaviness as, for example, going through an Earth experience may help to accelerate the process of becoming light, rather like going on a diet, I suppose! When Jesus talked about himself as being the light of the world he was using light in its widest meaning of full understanding, full acceptance, full freedom of spirit, not weighed down by any darkness of bigotry or intolerance or false pride or false humility or any restrictive emotion. "Let there be light" is the best wish that one can make on behalf of all. So a lot of what I say will be devoted to spreading light into dark corners.

God, the Animating Force

In talking about God I immediately run into the limitations of language. God is not a person so I cannot say "He" or "She." I don't want to use the word "It" either because it's not expressive enough. At the risk of being more than usually repetitive I'll use the word "God" where normally "He," "She," or "It" might suffice.

Each of us is a part of God, that is, the spirit beings that we are. So God is at least the sum total of the parts. But God is more than the total of the parts.

Somewhere at the back of your mind there's a memory of having been told that God had no beginning and will have no end. Everything in the physical Earth plane points to beginnings and ends; day and night, sleeping and waking, birth and death. So the idea of infinity is alien to humanity and very difficult, if not impossible, for a human being to comprehend in all its grandeur. Yet, having said that, I have to go on to say that God is an infinity of spirit existing through infinity. In other words, God is not limited by any concept of time or space. Therefore we cannot think of God in terms of time or space or, consequently, beginning or end.

Then how did it all start; the world, etc.? In the sense that everything is contained in God, everything has always been. God is eternally creative, however, so the structure or format of things keeps changing. Thus nothing ever dies but evolves into something else. All creation evolved out of God as an expression of the love that God is. Each part of creation is infused with that love and in turn expresses it in a creative way. That's easy enough to understand, I think. You can think of examples such as an artist, a writer, a carpenter, a cook, or anybody who ever writes a friendly letter or says a kind word to anybody else, or grass growing, a flower blooming, a bee making honey, a cat purring, a dog licking your face or wagging its tail, or water flowing, a spider building its web, or a bird in its nest.

Of all our sessions this is the most difficult because I am trying to convey an understanding of the infinity of God in words which are themselves an expression of finite concepts. If you don't understand a word you look it up in a dictionary which gives its meaning in another word or other words; then the word has a meaning for you which is related to your own limited understanding or experience of what the other word or words convey. I will attempt to make myself understood in simple terms. At the same time I want to remind you that when communication is reduced to words, unanimity as to the interpretation of the words is rarely achieved.

The most comprehensive and I hope most comprehensible definition of God I can give is this: God is an infinity of spirit, who has existed and will continue to exist through infinity. God is the source of all creativity, the life force of all creation, whose inspirational creativity never ceases nor ever will cease, who cannot be contained or confined in any limited or finite idea such as a person, place, or thing. All creation, and each bit of creation individually, is a part of God, but it cannot be said that God is the sum of all creation because that would be putting a limit to God and there is no limit. Each part of God has a share in God's infinite creativity; above all else, God is love, infinite love.

The word "love" conveys many different things to people. It's a much used and, I suppose I could say, much abused word. It's probably one of the most frequently used words of all. It's used in connection with a feeling a man may have for a woman or a woman for a man, which may be a thing of romance or of passion; or the feeling a person of one sex may have for a person of the same sex, which may have nothing to do with homosexuality or may indeed be a homosexual thing; or the feeling a parent may have for a child or a child for a parent; or the feeling friends may have for each other; or the feeling a person may have for an animal or an animal for a person; or the feeling a person may have for a possession, or an activity, or an experience; or the feeling a person may have for the God he envisages, or for a saint. It may be taken to mean anything from lust to ecstasy of a mystical kind. The wide variety of meanings given to it is a useful thing to bear in mind when you are trying to visualize the all-embracing concept of God. Every person has experienced and continues to experience love in different ways within the variety of meanings assigned to it. If a person says he loves someone or something he is giving expression to a feeling in a way that makes sense to him at a particular point in time.

When I say that God is love, then, what do I mean? I mean that God is the animating force in all expression that includes all life and all activities of life. I know what you're asking; surely not all activities of life, for example, wars, murders, oppression, rape, torture? Or the creation of an ugly-looking beast like the hippopotamus? Or irritating insects like fleas? Bear with me for a minute when I say that all life and all activities of life without exception are part of the positive expression of love. In other words, there is no evil. There is apparent evil and to human eyes many people act in such a way and many things are done which can only be described as bad or evil. For instance, how can I say to a mother whose daughter is raped that the force of love animates the man who performed the act of rape and the act of rape itself? Yet, that is the reality. Let me give you an example. A man and a woman meet, are attracted to each other and decide to get married. They have two children, a boy and a girl, both of whom they love very much. Time passes and the children grow up. The boy, now a young man, becomes part of a particular group which indulges in a lot of violent activities, including robbery and rape. The young man participates fully in the group's activities. In the meantime, his sister has channeled her life into a positive stream of respect and helpfulness towards all the people with whom she comes into contact. His parents are worried as a result of their son's behavior. They remember him as an innocent child and they wonder where they went wrong in his upbringing. They talk to him, pray for him, but apparently without success. They continue to love him even as he continues to reject them. In due course the father dies and some time later the mother also passes on. The son had lost all contact with them by this time. He is now much older and by his way of life he has become a coarse and brutal man. Much of his life is spent in recurring prison stretches. In the fullness of time he dies violently as he had lived. Meanwhile the remaining member of the family, his sister, had joined an order of nuns; she lived a most exemplary life and died surrounded by the love of her community.

On the face of it, three of the four people in that family unit were good people and lived positive lives. There is no difficulty in regarding them and their activities as animated by the force of love. The son, however, was apparently an evil man and performed evil deeds during most of his life on Earth. The problem is to accept that the same force of love as animated his parents and sister animated both him and his activities.

If you get a bad boil in your leg the treatment will probably be to lance it and let all the badness out. Love operates in somewhat the same way. The son in my case history had, by the exercise of his free will, built up a reservoir of negativity within himself as a spirit being which the love that he was and is forced out of him during that particular lifetime. The same force of love operating within the recipients of his acts of violence corrected by his acts an imbalance which earlier acts of free will on their part had created in them. He also helped his parents and his sister by creating in them, because of their love for him, a tolerance and a compassion which it would not be possible for them to feel had they not come up against the conflicts which he caused in them by the intimacy of his relationship with them. The very extent of his violence should in due course produce for him a remedial effect in a somewhat similar way to a sharp slap administered to a hysterical person. The old saying that things must get worse before they get better is very relevant in certain circumstances.

In the case history given, there was a lesson to be learned for each of the four people involved. But if God (or love) is the animating force in every person and thing, how come the process of apparent evil ever became necessary; in other words, that love seems to express itself in a seemingly unloving way? Because contrast is necessary for a full appreciation of life. The person who has never experienced cold cannot fully appreciate heat. The person who has never been thirsty or hungry cannot fully appreciate drink or food. A landscape artist would find very little expression in his painting if there were no clouds or shadows to counterbalance or highlight clear skies and light. A playwright's work would be very dull if there were no conflict in it. If you didn't know the feeling of anger you couldn't fully appreciate the value of serenity. The people who have lived through a war are almost invariably the ones who treasure peace most. A person who has never experienced pain cannot reach a full appreciation of the state of freedom from pain. Life on Earth is a learning experience designed to bring the person going through it to a fuller perception of the spirit being that he is. He is, in fact, undergoing a series of training courses geared to the raising of his awareness and consciousness levels. Because of his free will it is up to himself how he responds to the training. But the love within him, indeed the love that he is, will keep on throwing up situations and experiences until he has learned all the lessons he needs to learn to reach the full awareness of that love.

So then things aren't what they seem to be. It is well said that you should never judge the book by the cover.

Now the question asks itself; if all this is so, if all the bad as well as the good experiences of Earth existence are part of a broad design of love operating to achieve awareness of itself, how did that same design of love ever allow the state of stunted awareness to come about? That's a big question and I'll have to devote a separate session to it so as not to let this session become too diffuse. I'll confine myself at this stage to saying that a certain number of individual souls, a segment of God if you like, by the exercise of their free will allowed their awareness to become obscured to such an extent that in some cases it has seemed to become almost non-existent. (We're back to the poor hippopotamus and the flea again!) The force of love could not allow this to continue; it isn't possible for it to negate itself or any part of itself, and so began the long journey back to self-realization. Some souls have still to start the journey, others have made it all the way back, and the rest are at various stages in between.

Much of the teaching about God has centered on a divinity concentrated in three persons, Father, Son, and Holy Spirit. As I have said, God cannot be identified in personal terms except in the sense that God is present in all persons. Therefore, God cannot be confined in three persons unless they are seen as representing all life. I would suggest that it would be very helpful to use the symbolism of the Father in terms of those souls who never lost, or have regained, their self-awareness. The Son, symbolically, are those who are still at the start of the journey or who have not yet mastered the lessons of Earth. And the Holy Spirit are those who are helping others to find their way; for example, spiritual helpers or guides or guardian angels, whatever you wish to call them. In this way, the chain of cooperation running through all life can be easily seen.

"Who Made the World?"

It's a simple but rather unsatisfying answer to give to somebody asking, "Who made the world?" to say that God did and after that to depend on mystery or faith for further answers.

You have seen it postulated that dinosaurs dominated the Earth for 140 million years and that they became extinct about 65 million years ago. So the world is a pretty old place on that evidence.

I would like to convey as simply as I can why and how the physical world came into existence. I'm not going to go into scientific explanations, I'm merely going to state the facts in a bald sort of way.

God is love. Expression evolved out of love into individual parts each with full free will. The process of evolution is within a time sequence in your terms and I'll explain it on that basis, although I would just mention that time does not exist in the real world of spirit. However, in the physical world you operate within a time frame and that's your reality while you're there so there's no point in giving you details in a way that doesn't fit your concept of reality.

Over a million billion years ago (with a billion equaling a million millions; so long ago that there's no point in trying to put a time scale on it) the evolution into individual parts that I mentioned above happened. Each part, or soul, was spiritually equal to every other soul; each was equally endowed with the spirit of God (or love). The number of souls who thus evolved was a billion billion billions (with a billion again equaling a million millions). I will go into the various evolutionary stages or vibrations later, and when I do I will try to convey a picture of what these souls were doing then and what most of them are still doing now in the state of full awareness. All were, of course, initially in that state.

Some billions of years after the expression into individual souls happened, one soul decided that he would like to run the whole operation. In other words, he wanted to impose his will on all the other souls. During a period of about 50,000 years, he managed to get the support of roughly one percent of all souls, which was a small proportion, but a lot of souls, in his quest for dominance; they were prepared to subordinate their wills to his. (Incidentally you can see now that the proportion used by Jesus when he talked about there being more joy in heaven over one soul who was lost being found than over ninety-nine already saved, or words to that effect, was not a randomly chosen one.) He is commonly known as Lucifer. He drew around him an inner circle, each of whom in turn formed his own inner circle, and so on, so that within a relatively short period of time he established a hierarchy of which he was the head. This development was entirely incompatible with the true nature of spirit but it's an interesting pointer to the importance of free will in the scheme of things. Lucifer by his desire for power used his free will to influence others; they of their own free will allowed themselves to be influenced. At the same time others who had not allowed themselves to be influenced were unable to interfere because of their respect for free will.

When Lucifer found that he couldn't extend his influence any further he decided that he would isolate himself, with his supporters, from the others. It will hardly come as a surprise to you to learn that there was no great battle of the heavens. Again, this would have been incompatible with respect for free will.

Once respect for free will was breached in Lucifer's case, and in the case of all his supporters (who didn't respect their own free will in allowing it to become subordinate to his), there seemed to be nothing to stop it being breached again and again. Eventually the stage was reached where some souls had lost all awareness of their real selves and had become like zombies.

The souls who had not allowed themselves to be influenced by Lucifer observed, with great concern, what was happening. The link of love running through all spirit meant that what was happening to one was happening to all. Out of that concern evolved the world as a system which would provide a means by which lost souls could regain their awareness. In talking about the world I mean the whole universe; sun, moon, stars, planets, including Earth. Existence on Earth is only one of many learning experiences provided for souls.

Everything on Earth is infused with love; for instance, grass, water, stones; but such things aren't souls. They evolved in the Earth scene to help sustain life in physical form so that souls could stay in the Earth vibration.

Life on Earth can be categorized into two forms: stationary, in the sense of not capable of moving around, and non-stationary. Stationary life includes plants, trees, grass, flowers. Non-stationary life includes birds, insects, fish, animals, and human beings. Stationary life, while animated by love, is not soul. Non-stationary life is.

That brings me to the dinosaurs and other life of that kind. I mentioned that many souls lost all awareness of their real selves. They were literally lost. The spirit of love operating through the souls who had not lost their awareness developed a design of existence on Earth related to the state of awareness or non-awareness of souls at a particular point in time; hence the proliferation of insect, bird, fish, animal life. It's all a progression through to man which is the highest state of awareness (although often not obviously so) on the Earth plane.

But what of Lucifer? He had already lost self-awareness by his desire for dominance. The negative progression or regression continued in his case until he too was caught up in the general loss of identity. It is entirely mistaken to think of him as a prince of devils seeking to win over any souls he can for his kingdom of hell. He is as much a part of God as any other soul; he just simply lost his awareness of who and what he was. He has long since regained his lost position and he is now truly a bearer of light to those who are still in need of it.

I referred to non-stationary life being soul. If I may, I'll take the example of the hippopotamus and the flea. Each of these has lost all awareness of its real self. It's a strange and probably repulsive idea to think of a soul being housed in the body of a flea, not to mention that of a hippopotamus. Traditional teaching in Western countries is generally to the effect that only human beings have souls (as distinct from *being* souls). That's not correct.

But, you say, think of all the millions and millions of insects alone; how could each one be a soul? Here's where we come up against another complication. There was nothing to stop individual souls from expressing themselves into parts in the same way as did God. This didn't happen with the souls who never lost their awareness, precisely because they hadn't lost their awareness; they saw the total grand design of love and wouldn't interfere with it. But it did happen with the other one percent some of whom saw it as a means of increasing their numbers until eventually they would outnumber the ninety-nine percent. So they evolved into parts, and the parts in turn evolved into parts, and so on. At this stage the original souls were already in a state of diminished awareness. The process of diminution was intensified as the parts multiplied until some reached the point of no awareness at all. Thus you might have millions of fleas who house parts of one original soul, the soul comprising the whole lot. It wouldn't be accurate to call this a group soul; it's one soul that diffused itself into millions of parts. As awareness increases the parts begin to reintegrate until eventually the complete soul is ready to experience existence housed in a human body.

That's the broad pattern that I have outlined as simply as I can. I was one of the one percent, so were you, so were all the souls who have been through an Earth experience and others who have not, and so were the dinosaurs! It's hard to believe that we were so foolish, but we were. I have been fortunate enough to have found my way back to full awareness and now that I know the joy of it again, it is my dearest wish that all the others of the one percent should regain their original state as quickly as possible.

How many of the one percent have already gotten back? It's a long process and not many have yet made it all the way, but roughly half are well on the way.

Could it all happen again? Yes, of course, given free will. I think, however, that the experience of the one percent will be enough to prevent a repeat performance.

Infinity

I would like to say a little more about the infinity of God, which is such a difficult idea to grasp. There is no limit to

God. It follows that there is no limit to each soul as part of God, that each soul shares in the infinity of God.

Each soul is an infinite part of God, but God is more than the sum of all souls at any given time. God has a capacity for unlimited expression. There is nothing in existence or nothing will ever exist that has not been, or will not be, an expression of God.

I think it's not too difficult to comprehend that God will have no end (which means also, of course, that each soul will have no end). The real mystery about infinity is the no beginning part.

If you imagine the Earth completely covered by water with no physical boundaries of any kind you can get some tangible concept of infinity. But, of course, water is obviously a physical substance that had a beginning.

Light, in the sense of non-darkness, is another example. Light can be perceived but not seen by the human eye. It's obvious that it's there and when it's there. But, again, light has an apparent beginning.

Reason tells you that somewhere along the line everything must have a source. But reason can't make any deduction as to how the original source came to be there except to say that it must be rather like a recurring decimal; a source has a source has a source indefinitely.

Reason can, however, take us part of the way. How does anything get created? Take a poem, for example. The first thing that happens is that a person gets a feeling that he wants to write a poem about something, then the feeling expresses itself into thought and the poem follows. The feeling comes first, the thought gives expression to the feeling and the act of creation follows. So it is with all creation. Accordingly, the original source must have been a feeling.

But how did the feeling happen? Here, I'm afraid, is the crunch. I don't know the answer. And I can't find out the answer because it is not known. In other words, this is the ultimate question to which there is no answer, or the only answer to which can be that the feeling had no beginning.

I realize the implications of what I'm saying. How can I describe God as an infinity without beginning or end if I can't explain how God had no beginning? The best I can do is the following. A soul cannot lose its capacity for feeling. It may lose its awareness of its capacity, but not the capacity itself. I feel, therefore I am, eternally. The capacity has not changed, or I should say remains always the same; it is not subject to change. If it is not subject to change it cannot ever not have existed or ever not exist.

I know that this is an incomprehensible idea when considered in the light of a linear time sequence, but if you can conceive of time in the round, an eternal present, it's not so difficult to grasp.

In my description of God I said that, above all, God is "love," infinite love. As a description of God I like *love* best within the all-embracing meanings of that word, although a less ambiguous description would be "feeling and all its expressions."

Now, having arrived at the description of God as feeling and all its expressions, I need to go back to my earlier statement that God is more than the sum of all souls. Does this mean that with each soul forming part of God, all souls together still form only part of God? This question embraces the relationship of creation to its creator. If God is feeling and all its expressions, then God as well as being creator is also creation. So God is all, as all is infinitely; in other words, all souls and all their expression infinitely. Feeling continues to express itself eternally in souls as creator(s) and their acts as creation.

In this context, it might be well to consider the relationship of a poem to its creator. Once a poem is written it has its own existence. However, its content is still one with (the mind of) its creator. In a sense, it's an extension of him. Even though at some stage it may be destroyed or changed it still exists in a timeless dimension in its creator.

To take another example: the human body is the most common form of creation. While there are physical agents, the father and mother, the design of each human body is the choice of the soul which will require it for a time; effectively, each soul creates the body or bodies which it needs for life on Earth. Again, the body has its own existence but it also is at one with its creator. Even though it changes through the years until it eventually dies and disintegrates, each stage of its existence is in one way or another embedded in the awareness of its creator.

Creation, then, has its own existence, but its existence is essentially not separate from that of its creator; rather, in a real way, it is contained in it. Thus God is both creator and creation (actual and potential creation), feeling and all its expressions; in one word, love.

The Grand Design

It is my primary intention to provide an understanding of the whole scheme of life with suggestions as to how to derive as much benefit as possible from life on Earth.

Some of this material may be a bit difficult to absorb and to try to put into words, so don't be impatient if progress is slower than you'd like it to be.

In your world at the present time there is a great emphasis on doom and gloom. And, indeed, in an earthly sense it is difficult not to be gloomy. Things such as unemployment, taxes, inflation, drug abuse, poverty, crime, hostility between nations and within nations, are all constantly brought to attention either through personal experience or through the media or both. To somebody who is unaware of, or cannot accept, the continuity of life the whole outlook must appear rather grim.

Side by side with these depressive elements, however, there are positive indicators of progress, even in human terms. For example, there is less worldwide discrimination than ever before, both racially and sexually. More attention is being focused on the unequal distribution of wealth and more attempts are being made to do something about it. Society generally has become more egalitarian and less hypocritical in its attitudes. Authoritarianism seems to have had its day; people are respected more for what they are than for the positions they hold. Generally, there is more respect for the individual and for his right to live his life in his own way.

If the whole situation is looked at from orthodox points of view it may be logical to conclude that the forces of good and evil have both gained and are gaining strength and seem to be heading for an inevitable confrontation.

There are, of course, more people now on Earth than there ever were before. More and more souls are taking on physical bodies to try to speed up their spiritual development. This, as with any changing pattern, has inevitably caused disruption and an acceleration of trends towards harmony and disharmony.

⁓ I'd like to begin with a brief summary of *The Grand Design*. Each soul is a part of God. Roughly one percent of souls lost awareness of this and what it means. The other ninety-nine percent worked out a grand design of evolutionary growth to help the one percent regain their lost awareness. As souls evolve on their way back to full awareness they play their part in the implementation of the design. No soul, no happening, nothing at all, is overlooked within the framework of the design. Earth in all its aspects with all life on it is part of the design. Life on Earth is a learning experience aimed at growth in awareness. Each soul has free will to choose how it will live its life. The grand design is infinitely flexible and adjusts itself to the vagaries of free will so that even if a soul regresses spiritually in a particular lifetime it will be provided with other learning opportunities to redress the balance and to resume its climb up the ladder of awareness. Each soul has, if it wishes, evolved souls available to it to guide it during a lifetime and to help it achieve whatever purpose it has planned to achieve in that lifetime. No soul can be lost because that would be negation of its nature as part of God. At the same time, many souls are experiencing a lot of pain and trauma in trying to regain their former awareness. Those souls who never lost or have already regained full awareness or are well on their way towards achieving that end are ceaselessly trying to reduce the pain and trauma while being very careful not to interfere in any way with individual free will.

The state of the world today, then, is a direct result of the operation of free will. But the grand design has kept on accommodating itself to that free will and there is certainly no danger of failure on the part of the design. The fact that unquestioning acceptance of traditional beliefs is no longer operative for many people has been seen by some as an indication of failing standards or decreasing virtue. It isn't so, of course. Spiritual progress is only possible for any individual when he questions his beliefs and establishes his own truth, which may or may not be in accordance with his beliefs. (I don't mean to imply that he should necessarily change his beliefs: what I'm stressing is that he should understand them and be in harmony with them for himself.) The possibilities for growth in awareness for mankind in general are now greater than they have ever been. Unfortunately, however, growth doesn't happen without turmoil of one kind or another. It is necessary to bear in mind that Earth and the things of Earth are ephemeral and are only of importance in so far as their spiritual effect is concerned.

I said that all creation stems from feeling which defines itself in thought, and that all this is a continuing process without beginning or end. Feeling is therefore the Source, and all expression has evolved and continues to evolve out of it. Since feeling is constant and unchanging in itself, although continuously evolving in its expression of itself, it must always have been and continue to be. Where there is no such thing as time, this is not such a difficult concept; think of a circle, which has no beginning or end, rather than a straight line, which has both.

I realize that, to somebody who is conditioned to believing in a personal God as the Source of all, the idea of the source being something as apparently nebulous as feeling may, on the face of it, be outrageous and sacrilegious. Yet God is often spoken of in orthodox teaching as being love, which can only be described as feeling and/or expression of feeling.

God or love or feeling expressed itself into individual souls. Each soul has its own style which gives it its individuality, but the link of feeling or love binds all souls and all their creativity and acts of creation into one unlimited whole. Thus it is that no soul can indefinitely prevent itself from manifesting its true nature (feeling or love).

If feeling expresses itself in individual souls, and in individual persons in human terms, could there not be one Supreme Soul or Being or Person as the binding force? There could be in theory if that was the way feeling chose to express itself. But in reality it couldn't have so chosen; it would have been contrary to its nature, a diminution of feeling or love, to have expressed itself other than equally. The equality of all souls, no greater or lesser, is a fundamental characteristic of feeling, or love. As I explained in an

18

earlier session, the fall from awareness of the one percent of souls happened because they were untrue to their own natures and sought predominance over their fellow souls. Once there is a ruler, no matter how benevolent, and subjects, freedom is limited both for the ruler and the subjects. Feeling, or love, has to be perfect democracy if it is to be true to itself.

I have said that feeling is constant and unchanging in itself. When it expressed itself in individual souls did that not represent a change? It would have, had it expressed itself other than equally. But because it expressed itself equally there was no change in itself (its nature or style, if you like); the change is only in the way it expressed itself.

Suppose, for the sake of illustration, that we look on feeling and individual souls as creator and creation, and suppose that initially we narrow the idea of creator and creation down to a poet and the poetry he writes. Hasn't something been added; i.e., the poetry, to creation? If we broaden the idea, are all the individual souls not an extension of feeling, and is there still a central feeling which is a constant although not manifesting itself as one Being? Central to these questions is whether creation is in essence separate from its creator. It is not and cannot be. While it is a fact that the poetry has been added to creation, it is still a part of its creator, his expression of himself. Its essence is the feeling (which expresses itself in thought and then words) which went into its creation. This feeling cannot be something separate from the poet himself.

Two artists paint faithful reproductions of a particular landscape, yet the paintings will not make identical impressions on the viewers. What is it that makes the difference? Surely it is the feeling which is the essence of the creations (the paintings) which are themselves expressions of the artists.

Feeling is, of its nature, participative. If one part of itself remained separate from its expression into individual souls the whole beautiful concept of equality and unlimited expression in accordance with absolute free will could not have been realized. There can only be a central force or feeling in the sense that all are one.

Here I'd like to remind you of the symbolism of the Father who represents all the souls who never lost or have regained full awareness. The Son represents those souls who have still not reached acceptance of themselves and their place in the whole scheme of things (who haven't progressed beyond the second stage of evolutionary growth). And the Holy Spirit represents the souls who have evolved beyond the lessons of Earth and are now helping others to reach their level before they themselves move on to the ultimate state. When this symbolism is used, unity with the Father, which means unity without loss of individuality, is the ideal for all souls, and help is constantly flowing from the Father in order to make that ideal a reality.

I think it may be helpful to record the following analogy. Think of the soul as an electric light bulb which is perfect but which is buried in earth. If the bulb were to be switched on it wouldn't show any light. However, when the earth is removed and the bulb is completely clean it shows all its light. Yet it is exactly the same bulb, perfect when buried in earth and perfect when the earth is removed. So it is with each soul. It will show its perfection when it sheds its unawareness, but the unawareness only clouds that perfection; it doesn't and cannot destroy it.

Incidentally, in giving the example of an electric light bulb to illustrate a point, and in using words like perfection, I'm aware that I'm getting into limitations of structure. Perfection as a word implies a state where everything stops; no going beyond it. In the ultimate state of awareness there's no such thing as perfection in that sense—which would be very boring anyway—just stagnation; rather, it is a state of continually evolving consciousness. So the perfection which each soul will show as it sheds its unawareness will not be dull, or boring, or stagnant. It will be without limitation of any kind.

The world of spirit is vast and varied. Many souls on the journey back to full awareness are at different levels of awareness. Those at higher levels are helping those below them on the ladder; help is flowing all the way down from the Father. There is a coordination of effort within the grand design. Some souls have agreed to act as coordinators. For this reason they may seem to be ranked higher than others and since the coordinators at one level are themselves being coordinated at another level, and so on, you can see how there could appear to be a hierarchical spirit structure.

There is also the fact that the higher a soul's level of awareness, the more this is reflected in the aura of radiance it manifests. A soul, at, say the second stage coming into contact with a soul at the fourth stage will readily assume that that soul is a higher being than itself. The road to self-acceptance is a long and difficult one for most souls and involves finding comprehensive and satisfying answers to such questions as: Who am I? How did I come to exist? What is my place in the whole scheme of things? What is my relationship to others? There is no place for false pride or false humility in self-acceptance.

Religion

Religion is an emotive subject and I hope that anything I say will tend to eliminate emotions rather than encourage them. However, religion is a matter of fundamental interest to souls so I will discuss it in depth.

How did religion come about in the first place? As a result of the fall from awareness souls lost sight of their greatness as parts of God. Under the grand design, help was made available to them in many different ways, notably inspiration and the example of advanced souls. In due course souls began to realize that it was possible to get help from higher sources. In so-called pagan times there were many gods who were worshipped as higher beings by people forming themselves into groups. Joyful happenings came to be seen as signs of favor on the part of a god or gods and occasions of sorrow were marks of godly displeasure which called for placatory offerings or sacrifices. Thus the ethos of reward and punishment grew; reward for behavior thought to be pleasing to the gods and punishment for behavior thought to be offensive to them.

Later religions concentrated their worship on one god, but the concept of a higher being who dispensed reward and punishment remained and still remains.

Religions were born out of the felt need for worship of apparently unpredictable and arbitrary higher power(s). From time to time people emerged who considered that a new truth or the whole truth had been revealed to them by God. Others came to share their conviction and in due course organizations were built around them. Thus the world now has a multiplicity of religions and religious organizations.

I don't wish to understate in any way the benefits and the divisions which religions have brought to mankind. They have at one and the same time provided great comfort to people in need of it, and restriction of freedom on people least likely to be able to cope with restriction. They have given answers with great authority and sheltered people within the ambit of that authority. Conformity brings salvation, nonconformity may lead to damnation, all expressed in terms of eternity! That religions have encouraged, often imposed, desirable codes of behavior between people can-not be denied any more than that they have also encouraged and often imposed penal codes on those not of their per-suasion. Men bonded together in a common cause tend to behave with savagery, albeit sometimes of a polite kind, towards those who do not agree with them.

All religions play a part in the grand design. Bear in mind that Earth and its experiences are there for learning purposes. Religions provide many learning opportunities; for example, cooperative effort, community living, thought-fulness towards others, respect for others, working towards higher ideals. The fact that there are so many religions is an encouragement of tolerance, although the reverse is often the case, in that it is at least an indication that there may be many versions of truth and many ways to heaven. Even the very fact that religions or religious beliefs may be occasions of intolerance for some people may in the long run turn out to be a big help to those people; often it is only when extremes of behavior are reached that self-confrontation can no longer be avoided.

Is any one religion better than another as a stepping-stone to awareness? Not necessarily; they all have their uses and play their parts, as I have said. If a person is born into or becomes a member of a particular religion it is usually because he needs the learning opportunities which that reli-gion can best give him. The danger with religions is that their members may shelter behind rules and regulations and allow their thinking to be completely conditioned by those rules and regulations. It can be a very comfortable and com-forting feeling for a person to have everything mapped out for him; the rules are there, all he has to do is follow them and his future in eternity is assured!

Why should any person born into the security of an established religious framework which gives him a promise of eternal happiness if he lives according to its rules want to, or need to, question the basis of his beliefs?

Each individual soul is unique. It has its own special place in the jigsaw of life. All the parts (souls) fit into the whole and are ineluctably interlinked within the whole but they retain their individuality. Each soul is a combination of feeling and thought. It has to express itself in total balance of feeling and thought in the context of its own individuality before it can be said to have reached full awareness. If it allows any part of its feeling and thought to be done for it by another or others it is not possible for it to express its individuality fully.

What I am saying is that, while religions play their part and are helpful in many positive and negative ways for souls climbing the ladder of awareness, at some stage each soul must come to terms with itself as a unique entity and not just as a member of a particular religious organization. The lifeblood of a religious organization is that its members feel and think in the same way about its teachings; it has to be or it wouldn't survive as an organization. Obviously there's no room for individuality in more than a limited way in that situation. Accordingly, if a soul wants to continue to climb the ladder, it will, when it is ready to do so, abandon membership of organized groupings and find its own unique relationship with, and place within, all life. There are no religions at the seventh stage—in fact, there are no religions beyond the second stage—although there are, of course, former members of religious organizations which served their purpose as a means towards the end of increased awareness.

Awareness vs. Conformity

When a soul decides to reincarnate it automatically chooses to restrict the methods by which it can exercise free will. For a start, the pull of gravity on its physical body confines its freedom of movement. The combination of brain and memory restricts its freedom of feeling and thought. And the environment into which it chooses to be born conditions it further by its laws and general behavioral characteristics.

Many people rebel against the constraints. Some keep on moving from place to place in the hope that they will eventually find a community and a lifestyle that they feel will suit them. Some stay where they are but dissociate themselves from all communal activities. Some seek change by political methods or by using the communications media or by any other means open to them. Some break the laws and manage to do so with impunity; or, if they get caught, are brought through the courts and fined or put in prison.

Most modern communities live under systems by which they periodically elect politicians as their representatives to govern them. The day to day business of state administration is conducted by public servants answerable to politicians, the representatives of the people. Inbuilt into the systems are means by which existing laws are enforced mainly through police, courts, and prisons, and new laws are made. Thus it transpires that the individual member of a community, depending on his attitude, may consider himself to be protected or victimized by the laws and procedures made and enforced on behalf of the whole community.

What ought the attitude of the aware soul, or the soul seeking growth in awareness, be to governmental systems? They are unquestionably aids to spiritual development in that they provide many learning opportunities. For example, how to cope with power at the administering and receiving end; how to sit in judgment on the actions of others without also judging them; how to respect the rights of others to their own space and their own ways of thinking; how to overcome prejudice and bigotry and intolerance generally; how to learn to be mentally free in the midst of restrictions while at the same time not imposing in any way on the freedom of others; how to begin to see reality in the midst of illusion. The aware person recognizes the systems for what they are, learning opportunities for spiritual growth, and uses them accordingly. He realizes that by having decided to reincarnate he has chosen restriction of an obviously concentrated kind for the limited duration of a lifetime. This restriction is designed to produce greater freedom in the long run, and there is no point in railing against the circumstances in which he finds himself if he considers them too constraining for him. What he does, ideally, is find out what he has to learn from his physical conditions and then make sure that he doesn't neglect the opportunities presented to him. By looking on the systems in this way he is not affected by them and doesn't take them too seriously. They are merely passing phases in history and have no importance in themselves; they are only important insofar as they serve as aids to spiritual growth.

Does this mean, then, that the aware person lives with the systems rather than seeking to change them? Not necessarily. Any change that will enable and encourage people to express themselves with greater individual freedom, and to respect the rights of others to do so, also aids the implementation of the grand design. It is of vital spiritual importance to each individual that he should learn to take responsibility for himself; that any institution (church or state) cannot do it for him. What I am talking about, of course, is spiritual responsibility, responsibility for what he feels and thinks, not material responsibility, which is of no ultimate significance in itself. Conservative paternalistic systems by their nature don't encourage individual freedom of expression nor consequently the development of spiritual responsibility. Accordingly, the aware person is likely to be a radical rather than a conservative, but he doesn't confuse radicalism with fanaticism or obsessionalism. He works to create, or to help to create, a climate of freedom of thought, but he doesn't fall into the trap of dogmatism, of thinking that his answers are exclusively the right ones. At the risk of being accused of being dogmatic, I have to say that the aware person is never dogmatic! He may be firm in holding on to his own truths, but in expressing them he is careful not to try to impose his way of thinking on anybody else.

Letting Go

It is, perhaps, appropriate to discuss what I would like to call a "letting go" process. Within the physical Earth framework one cannot hold on to time. Day follows day, week follows week, month follows month, and year follows year relentlessly and inescapably. So a soul living within a physical body has to let go of each day, week, month, year. The trouble is that letting go, not just of time but of all the happenings, etc., during the passage of time, can be painful. Lost: youth, looks, virility, agility, sporting ability, opportunities for creative expression, remunerative employment, childbearing, etc.; physical faculties, such as sight, hearing; relationships with parents, children, spouses, relatives, friends, lovers, are but some examples of sources of pain which seem to be inseparable from the Earth experience. Given that time does not stop, neither can the process of aging, with all its physical implications, nor separation, with all its pain of loss. So how does one lessen the pain or, better still, find freedom from it altogether?

We have now come to a question that is central to the whole purpose of life on Earth.

Clearly, the grand design comprehended that human beings would become attached to each other and to many of the things, activities and attitudes which are inherent in the Earth experience; for example: food, drink, sex, clothes, gambling, reading, writing, painting, sculpting, sports, drugs, business, politics, conflict, religion, power, authority, making money, status, competition, illness, grievances, beauty, piety, duty, righteousness, judgment, sarcasm, morbidity, joylessness, inferiority and superiority complexes, and so on. The grand design also obviously envisaged that sooner or later detachment, non-attachment, would occur. Death of the body provides an enforced physical separation. This is intended to point the way towards detachment, or, as I prefer to call it, nonattachment. Life goes on. People have to continue to cope with the daily challenges somehow without the physical presence of their loved ones. They have to let go physically. If they can let go mentally, *while continuing to love*, then they are on the way towards accepting that they themselves are free spirits and, most important, all others are also.

In my view, letting go is a process of becoming, which sounds like a self-contradictory statement to make. In the interest of simplicity I'll use a personal approach. You believe that you are divine consciousness. You have not yet acquired the totality of that consciousness (or regained it, I should say); you are still rubbing off the earth of unawareness. Negativity does not and cannot coexist with divinity. Therefore, the more aware you become the more you let go. For example, if you are worrying about how you are going to find enough money to pay the electricity bill, you let go of the worry in the knowledge that divine consciousness never worries about anything and that the means of paying the bill will be present for you when needed.

Incidentally, there is a certain conditioning and, consequently, security about worrying. People are often considered to be lacking in feeling if they don't worry. An expected response is, or becomes, a form of security. Of course, worry is not alone a waste of energy, but, even worse, is a pressurizing thought form on the object of worry.

Divine consciousness does not need anything. There's no pain of loss because there is no loss. There's no pain of separation because there is no separation. When I talk of letting go I mean *letting go of unawareness into awareness.* The fundamental and *essential* starting point is acceptance that you and all souls are divine consciousness. Letting go of all fear into that consciousness follows in due course. Until it does you have not yet reached full acceptance of your divinity. Belief is not enough; it's an intellectual exercise only. Acceptance is totally spiritual; it is harmony of feeling and thought into consciousness.

Being Divine Consciousness

Each soul has God within, or, in other words, is love or divine consciousness. Assuming that you have no difficulty accepting that, either through your thoughts or your feelings, how do you contact the God within and thus be consciously divine while still also human? For a start, I suggest that you remind yourself constantly that you are divine consciousness temporarily using a physical framework. The more fully you accept that, the more you will manifest it without separation into a duality of human and divine or material and spiritual. Accordingly, there shouldn't be any question of contacting the God within, which implies separation, but, rather, of allowing yourself to be God, which means integration. That's easier said than done, of course, especially when you are faced with physical problems, such as illness, or relationship or financial difficulties. In such circumstances how do you actually manifest your divinity? Suppose you say to yourself "I am God," or, "I am love," or, "I am divine consciousness," and "God/love/divine consciousness does not have problems or difficulties;" what process should take place? Do you work through your feelings or your thoughts, or both, or do you see yourself as a spark or an expression of divinity letting go into the wholeness of divinity, or what?

I will refer now and then to the concept about being one with the Father, with the Father representing all the souls (the ninety-nine percent) who never lost awareness. This is a sweeping concept which, in the human condition, is difficult to imagine, rather like statements such as "All is one," "One is all" so let's try and break it down a little. You are an individual soul, and so is each and every soul. Yet, in a state of full awareness you are also one with each and every other soul and with all life. In terms of consciousness you are your own consciousness but you are also linked to the universal consciousness like a wave in the sea. The wave has all the qualities of the sea and is the sea but is not all the sea, yet it is all in the sense that it is inseparable from the sea and is in unity with it. (The sea is a limited analogy in that God is more than the sum of all the parts.)

So where are we? God is within you. You are, in fact, God (or love), but that's obviously not an exclusive proposition since each other soul is also God. In contacting God, accordingly, does that mean that you contact all consciousness, aware and at varying levels of unawareness? It could mean that, and that's why I suggest meditating on unity with the Father so that then you are merging with full awareness. Ultimately, of course, there will again be a unity of total awareness when all the souls still searching have found their way back to full awareness.

Now we come back to the method. Do you have to have an image in your mind before you can meditate? For instance, is it helpful to personalize the Father, or use symbolism such as the wave and the sea? In my view, using the symbolism would be a better approach than personalization since personalization implies a sense of separation and limitation. If a feeling of unity can be achieved without either personalization or symbolism, then that's the best way. Once you inject an image, whether a personalization or a symbolism, you are starting with an intellectualization from the outside in, rather than from the inside out. The source is feeling (love). Feeling is being. Feeling expresses itself into thought in the ideal balance of being. So, in my view, the best way to contact the God within is to let go of all thought as far as possible and simply to be, to let the love that you are take over. You can describe, rationalize, define through thought, but you cannot think yourself into being. The being (feeling) comes first, before the thought.

Suppose you are feeling happy. You start thinking about why you are happy. Then you have lost the *feeling* of happiness. You have circumscribed it, analyzed it, and changed it. Or you are listening to music, absorbing it into your being. You begin to wonder what it is, who composed it, etc. Again, you are now limiting the feeling. Or you are walking, feeling the peace of a quiet countryside. You start observing wild flowers, categorizing them, or trees, or whatever; once again you are channeling your feelings into a thought process of definition which may very well be enjoyable but is nonetheless a separation from the feeling of integration with the countryside.

You are conditioned by thought patterns. Your conditioning predisposes you to slot everything into patterns of what you know. Thus you constantly limit yourself. How do you know you have a problem? Because thought tells you so in its analytical, judgmental functioning. How to change that? You are faced with a situation which thought tells you (from its conditioning) is a problem. Suppose you are married, the sole breadwinner of a family of five, with a heavily mortgaged house, but with a level of salary which enables you and your family to enjoy a comfortable standard of living. You lose your job and have no immediate prospect of getting another one. The process of thought tells you that if you cannot get a job with relatively the same level of pay as your previous one, the standard of living of yourself and your family will have to be reduced considerably, not to mention the fact that your house will probably be repossessed by the financial institution which made the mortgage arrangement with you. No matter how you think about it, the answer is still the same; get a new, equally well paid job, or accept a drastically reduced standard of living. Thought puts you into a straitjacket of options.

So here is a concrete situation to put the question of contacting the God within to the test. My way of dealing with it would be to stop thinking about it altogether and hand it over to the divine consciousness that you are. Divine consciousness (God, love) will present a solution to you that will lead you into a new and expanded pattern of thought, if you let it. That sounds passive, but, in reality, it means that your guides will channel the energy of all evolved souls into solving your difficulty.

You are still somewhat puzzled about the method of contacting the God within or handing over to your divine consciousness. The difficulty is in trying to rationalize something that cannot be rationalized. So now you have created a problem for yourself. Stop thinking about the how and let go into the feeling of being love. Then you are at one with the God within and the question of making contact no longer arises.

But, you ask, in order to let go, don't I have to think about letting go? So, doesn't the process start with thought if only on the basis of thinking not to think? Ideally, feeling and thought are totally harmonious functions of mind (soul) and, accordingly, are not separate from each other. They only become separate when thought defines feeling in terms of conditioning. Suppose we look again at the situation of the person who lost his job. His conditioning influences his thinking in certain directions. Until he stops thinking about his problem he is restricting the possibilities of solving it into the limitations of his own thought patterns, influenced as they are by his subconscious mind. When he lets go into divine consciousness he allows himself to be free of his subconscious so that his feelings and thoughts can work in harmony, united in consciousness.

Words are an inadequate form of communication in this area because by their nature they define and, therefore, limit. I don't use words, as you know them, anymore as a means of communication. That's why this has been such a difficult session for you, since you have to deal in words. However, we have done our best.

God/Persons: Avatars

"Go forth and multiply," "Teach all nations," slogans such as these have been used throughout the centuries to encourage proselytism in one form or another. All sorts of methods have been used by people hell-bent (in a manner of speaking!) on converting others to their beliefs. Although I used the expression "hell-bent," tongue-in-cheek, it is appropriate to bring hell into the equation because, in general, the most earnest proselytizers have been, and are, motivated by total sincerity of purpose aimed at saving souls from an eternity of punishment. The saving aspect is usually emphasized, and, more often, it is saving *from* rather than saving *for*; the eternal punishment is more easily conceived or imagined than the eternal reward.

When Jesus came on Earth as Jesus, he had reached the state of accepting himself for what he was; God, or son of God, if you like. He had accepted his own divinity, but not in an exclusive sense; he had also and equally accepted the divinity of all souls. He wanted to share his consciousness, to help others to reach the acceptance that he had reached. So, if being saved is defined as being helped to reach a total state of consciousness, Jesus can suitably be called a savior. Although I can tell you that he would much prefer to be seen as an example, or a guide, or a fellow traveler, who found out what direction to take to get out of the by-roads on to the main road. He wants to relieve all others of the pain of getting lost and/or coming to dead ends time and time again.

Are there specially chosen ones, god/persons, or avatars, or whatever else they may be called? As we have already seen, all are equal in God, or, put another way, God is equally in all. The only inequality is in awareness. Many souls of advanced awareness have come, and still come, to Earth from time to time to try to help others. A common characteristic of all those souls is their true humility; they have come to an acceptance of themselves as God and all that that means and all that they are trying to do is to help all others find a similar acceptance for themselves. They do not look for devotion or worship or to be regarded as gurus; in other words, they don't set out to personalize themselves as God.

The various exhortations attributed to Jesus, such as, leaving father and mother and brother and sister for his sake, "Rise up and follow me," "Go, and sin no more," and statements, such as "I am the way, the life and the truth," are usually interpreted too literally. He was, of course, talking in a spiritual sense, pointing to himself as one who had achieved spiritual freedom or awareness, and emphasizing that this is the goal for everybody. He was drawing attention to the fact that in any relationship, no matter how intimate, it is necessary to achieve spiritual freedom (which may, or may not, mean physical separation). Spiritual freedom is a totality of expression through feelings and thoughts. You are a spiritual being, an expression of God, creator and created, what is and all that is, individual consciousness and collective consciousness, limited awareness (temporarily), and unlimited awareness. A soul will never be able to reach full awareness until it accepts completely all that is expressed in the last sentence above. Acceptance involves understanding, knowing, that what is so for one soul is also so for each and every soul without exception. Such acceptance has all sorts of implications, e.g., non-interference with free will, making no judgments, non-possessiveness. What a soul accepts for itself, it accepts for each and every other soul. It follows that there is no dependency, in a spiritual sense, no attachment except in a loving way, letting go, setting free. There are no hooks, no chains, in spiritual freedom.

Christianity

Christianity is founded on the belief that God sent his only son to become man and to be crucified, thereby taking on himself the sins of mankind and by his death and resurrection opening the gates of heaven to redeemed man. God is the Creator, a separate Being. Man is the created, made in the image of God but wholly inferior to Him.

During the 1900-plus years since its foundation, Christianity has found expression in different religions, but has retained its belief in the separation of God from man, of creator from creation.

In our sessions I have emphasized the oneness of God and man, the unity of creator and creation. A Christian reading the records of our sessions is faced with a dilemma. If his reason and/or his knowing tell him that my outline contains truth for him, his belief in orthodox Christianity must be shaken since, on the face of things, there seems to be no way in which the two positions can be reconciled.

Fundamentally, Christianity, as it has developed, does not reflect the teachings of Jesus Christ. However, nothing happens by accident. It was a part of the grand design that Jesus came on Earth and taught as he did. Equally, it was a part of the grand design, continually adjusting itself in line with the effects of free will, *that his teachings should have been interpreted as they have been since his time on Earth.*

Again I must repeat myself: life on Earth is a learning experience. The events of Earth, the happenings, the teachings are in themselves, or in isolation, unimportant. They assume importance because of the effects they create on the awareness of individual souls. Thus it is that, for instance, you can change your past, not because you can change the events in your past, but because you can change the effects they had on you.

By and large, people have not believed in themselves. They wanted to believe in a power outside of themselves that regulated birth and death and much of what happened in between. Orthodox Christianity met that need; if the need did not exist Christianity would not have developed the way it did.

The sole object of the grand design is to help souls to raise their awareness levels to the stage where they will no longer need help. The design is *infinitely flexible* and responsive in the means by which it provides help. If you want to believe in an external force regulating your life, then you will be helped within your pattern of belief. You will also be helped in your pattern of nonbelief if you choose not to believe in anything beyond life on Earth.

Jesus spoke much of his oneness with the Father. He also impressed on his listeners that they could be as he was. For later generations, he became identified with the Father in oneness of Father and only Son whereas, of course, what he was teaching was the oneness, in common with him, of all souls with the Father. He became the redeemer, the intercessor with the Father, the apparently human but really not human face of God. In order to preserve the idea of his separateness from humanity, the concept that God could not become an ordinary human being, his birth, death and resurrection were portrayed as miraculous events contrary to the natural order of things.

There is no doubt but that Christian beliefs, as they have evolved, have helped more souls to raise their levels of awareness, at least by providing a consciousness of continuing life, than if the teachings of Jesus had been interpreted as he intended them to be at the time he outlined them. Otherwise the grand design would have found ways of correcting the misinterpretations. Is this not in some way making a mockery of Jesus? No. His level of awareness was such that he knew who and what he was. His purpose was to help others to reach his state. They did not believe in themselves as he believed in himself. Because of the certainty of his belief in himself and the aura of understanding that he conveyed, they exalted him since they felt that they could not be as he was. He was true to himself, therefore he could not be mocked or belittled in any real way. He fulfilled his purpose; it is unimportant that it was fulfilled in ways that he did not himself envisage during his life on Earth.

In spite of what might be taken as appearances to the contrary, souls are progressing through the various stages of development at an increasingly faster rate. Much of the apparent chaos and turbulence of modern life is a reflection of the inadequacy of traditional beliefs as they are now perceived. Those beliefs still play their part and will continue to do so but on an ever-decreasing scale. It is like the storm before the calm rather than the other way around. More and more souls are searching for beliefs with deeper meaning for themselves. Ultimately their search will only end when they accept with an inner realization that knows no contradiction that they are one with all life and with the source of all life.

Total acceptance of oneness rather than separation is the key that opens the door to progression beyond a certain level of awareness.

Second Coming

From the beginning of Christianity, what has been popularly called the Second Coming has been debated. It has been variously associated with a Final Judgment Day and with renewals of spirituality. One way or another it has been generally believed by those who adhere to Christianity that Jesus will come again to Earth in some form.

Of course, there will be no Judgment Day, final or otherwise. Ultimately, however, there will be a time of great rejoicing when all souls will have regained full awareness. This will not be nirvana, or nothingness; on the contrary, it will be wholeness of individuality as part of the wholeness of wholeness. I make no predictions as to when that time will come; in one sense it is already here, given the grand design; in another, it is a long way off, given free will.

What gave rise to the belief in a Second Coming was the fact that while Jesus ostensibly came to save the world, it was obviously not saved by the time he left it. On one level then, it was an apparently logical thing that he should have left his teachings after him; given souls a chance to receive and follow them and eventually sit in judgment on them; taken those who faithfully followed his teachings with him to eternal happiness in heaven, and condemned those who failed to do so to eternal damnation in hell. On another level, it was also logical that he would wish to come again to finish what he had started, to implement such a massive spiritual renewal that all would be saved the next time round.

It is a downgrading of the nature of any individual soul to believe that it can be saved (to use the common terminology) by any act or series of actions of another, no matter how meritorious. There is no escaping from the fact that each soul has to find its own salvation; in other words, its own wholeness of awareness. It can be, and is, helped, of course, but no amount of help is of any use to it unless it receives it and reacts to it in a positive way.

I don't exclude the possibility that Jesus will at some stage decide on another earthly experience, not as a savior but in order to help others to help themselves. I can tell you that it is not at present envisaged by the grand design that he should do so and I think it is most unlikely that he will since he has now progressed beyond the fourth stage.

In a totally spiritual sense, however, the concept of a Second Coming is very real. It is a continuum in that he is, of course, ceaselessly helping others. He has gone past the stage where it would be possible for him to pass judgment on any soul. Judgment is a feature of nonawareness.

Awareness and Non-awareness

The combination of non-awareness and free will has led and still leads souls into all sorts of difficulties. These difficulties can be variously classified as unhappiness, confusion, depression, phobias, obsessions, conflicts, cruelties, barbarities, intolerance, dogmatism, false pride, fanaticism, apathy, arrogance; each one in its own way constitutes a hell on Earth or beyond it, or, quite probably, in both situations.

There is no such place as hell in the sense of a place of eternal punishment for damned souls. Each soul creates its own hell; the hell that it creates on Earth may be just as bad as the hell that it creates beyond it.

There has been much lurid presentation of the tortures of hell. Like everything else, this serves a purpose if only in a negative way. Anything that makes people stop and think about themselves and where they are going can be helpful.

The polarization of a personal God with hordes of adoring angels and a personal Devil or Satan with legions of ministering devils was a logical consequence of the prevailing concepts of good and evil. Once good and evil were accepted as realities in total opposition to each other, it followed that there had to be a personification of all-good as the source and director of all-good, and a personification of all-evil as the source and director of all-evil, also in total opposition to each other. In that situation there could never be a reconciliation of the two forces. Both were, and are, seen to be locked in a continuing struggle for new recruits which will only be finally resolved on a day of judgment when those who have chosen God will join Him in eternal happiness in heaven; and those who have chosen Satan will share His eternal torment in hell. In the common delineation of the struggle, God as the personification of all-good, always fights fairly; but Satan, as the personification of all-evil, is prepared to stoop to anything, even to representing himself as God or one of His angels or saints. As a follow-up to this delineation, any communication from a spirit source is regarded as suspect; more than likely Satan or one of his minions up to his usual tricks.

As you will find, some will dismiss these writings as the work of Satan. The fact that I have said that there is neither evil nor devil will be represented as being exactly the kind of statement that suits Satan in that it gives him the freedom of the park, as it were, and people will not be on their guard against him. Although if there were such a being as Satan, so full of false pride as he is said to be, I doubt if he'd be prepared to agree, for whatever motive, to have himself and his Kingdom depicted as non-existent. Megalomaniacs are not notable for their self-effacement.

We have gone into this before and there is no way of proving in the context of these writings whether what I'm saying is true or untrue. If it is true, much traditional teaching is untrue unless it is seen in symbolical terms rather than as reality. I, and all who are cooperating with me on this venture, think it is time to replace the morality play, illusion, with reality. I am aiming what I'm saying at reason and beyond reason at the *knowing* within each soul. My representation of life is a totally inclusive one, or, if you like, a totally non-exclusive one. There is no place in my representation for Satan, all-evil, eternal devils, or eternal hell. God is all, all is God, and those souls who are not at present aware of that must eventually return to such awareness if they are ever to be truly themselves.

In the meantime some souls, due to the extent of their nonawareness, behave in such a way as to give, or to encourage the giving of, substance to the traditional beliefs about Satan and devils and evil. If their behavior is recognized for what it is—the result of nonawareness—they will be treated with far more compassion and understanding and more easily helped to see life in a different way. Ultimately it is not just they who will be helped, it is all souls. The restoration of complete harmony to life is a matter of vital significance for all souls, but especially, of course, for those who, in their unawareness, are most active in promoting disharmony.

Grace

Being in a state of grace is commonly equated with being free from sin. Grace is regarded as a gift from God, most powerfully conferred by sacraments; for example, the sacrament of baptism is said to free a child from original sin and thereby make it possible for it to get to heaven. (I should have said a person rather than a child, but people normally think of baptism in connection with children.)

The rite of baptism is symbolic. Think of sin as separation from self (or God). Original sin, then, was what gave rise to the initial separation, that is, the fall from awareness. Water is the material expression of spirituality. The pouring of water over the child signifies the spiritual nature of the child. It also signifies the cleansing of the child from what separates it from its true (spiritual) nature.

In ultimate terms, baptism is a ritualistic dramatization of what is inevitable, the regaining of full awareness or the attainment of heaven, whichever way you like to look at it. Unfortunately, however, baptism, or any sacrament, is only symbolic and does not, and cannot, have the miraculous power attributed to it. I say unfortunately because it would be a very easy shortcut if it had; but that would, of course, be an interference with the freedom of the individual soul. The existence of free will means that each soul makes its own choices, even if they lead to hell rather than heaven in terms of nonawareness as opposed to awareness.

Incidentally, do you think that people really believe in the power of baptism? If they do, why don't they wish that their children should die in infancy and thus be spared the risk of hell? And where does infinite justice fit into a situation where an infant who dies without having had an opportunity to commit sin may go straight to heaven through the power of baptism, and a person who survives to adulthood is faced with all sorts of occasions of sin and by succumbing to even one of them may go to hell for all eternity?

Yet religious rites, sacraments, etc., serve a purpose. They are signposts to the eternal nature of life. They point the soul towards a realization of its higher potential. They are a source of help to souls to shed burdens of guilt and worry and despair and loneliness. I don't mean to be frivolous when I say that they have been, and are, to many adults what Santa Claus is to many children, a reaching out of the imagination beyond all the bounds of rationality and an opening of the mind to things beyond the day-to-day routine of existence.

Even as it takes part in all the rituals, however, and no matter how wholehearted it is in the observance of them, the mind has an inner knowing that it is suspending a part of itself. For some time it will manage to still half-formed questionings with the much resorted-to answer that what cannot be explained is a mystery; with another part of the circle of non-answers being that a mystery is what cannot be explained. Eventually, however, the mind will not be satisfied with evasions and then it is really on the road to increased awareness. Anything that stimulates the mind to ask questions is helpful; thus also are the rituals a source of help, albeit an unconsciously indirect one.

I would define a state of grace as a feeling of oneness with all life, a harmonious condition in which all beings, things, happenings have their own place and are allowed to unfold themselves without interference. It is not a passive condition;

rather it is active in the most effective possible way in that it is flowing with life, the creativity of life, and not a frustrating misuse of energy in attempting to swim against the tide.

An illustration may be helpful. Unknown to each other, two men are traveling by train on the same journey. As all the seats are occupied they have to stand. Each of them has a rather heavy case with him. One man holds the case, changing it from hand to hand, for the duration of the journey, about an hour. He endures the journey impatiently and when he reaches his destination he is tired, his hands are sore, his case feels heavier than ever and he is generally in bad humor. The second man leaves his case on the floor and decides to enjoy the journey to the best of his ability. When his trip is over his case feels light and he is good-humored and relaxed.

This little story can be looked at in different ways. For example, the journey symbolizes a lifetime on Earth. Both men are born at the same time and die at the same time. The train is the spiritual help available to them all through life. The cases are the subconscious elements of their minds. The first man makes no use of the train (his spiritual help) in order to relieve him of the burden of his case (subconscious). By the time he reaches the end of the journey (dies) his case is heavier and he is in worse condition than he was when he decided to start the journey (reincarnate). The second man, however, uses the train to relieve him of the burden of his case. At the end of the journey the case is lighter and he is happier.

On another level, the train symbolizes the harmonious pattern of movement and change in all life. The first man endures it impatiently and gets no benefit from it. The second man flows with it and gets considerable benefit from it.

The second man is more likely to be in a state of grace, as I have defined it, than the first man.

The Bible

The Bible has everything known to the human condition; for example, devotion, power, mystery, grandeur, anger, judgment, lust, war, peace, pestilence, plagues, miracles, faith, hope, charity, cruelty, compassion, ruthlessness, destruction, birth, death, sickness, incest, rape, pillage, righteousness, intolerance, tolerance, greed, envy, insecurity, sacrifice, beauty, ugliness, fear, love.

By and large, the Old Testament is a story of harshness with an emphasis on fear, while the New Testament stresses compassion and love.

How did the Bible come to be written? Was it divinely inspired? How historically accurate is it?

The Bible is the product of many minds, some in spirit, some in physical bodies. The various parts of it were written over a long period of time and through different incarnations. Some souls worked on it both in spirit and in repeated physical incarnations; for example, Matthew, Mark, Luke and John, who later wrote the four Gospels of the New Testament, had earlier participated in the writing of the Old Testament. The various contributors set down the material as it came to them and did not envisage it forming part of a best-selling book. Others later combined to bring all the parts together, and the Bible as you know it came into being. The original writings were much transformed in the process by editing, re-editing, and translation. Changes were made in order to make the writings conform with current beliefs. The four Gospels, in particular, were subject to substantial editing, both to fit in with desired beliefs and to make them consistent with each other as far as possible.

Since everything is the work of God, since each soul is divine, the Bible was, of course, divinely inspired. Much of it is allegorical. The Old Testament should be seen in that way and not as a historical document. Yet there is a factual thread running through it. The evolution into the human state did start with two people. The models were already there from the first stage. Adam and Eve, as the two people have been called, did exist. As a matter of interest, Eve's body was not formed out of one of Adam's ribs but was created in its own right as the female model for the human race. All the other characters mentioned in the Old Testament also existed.

The description of Adam and Eve being banished from the Garden of Eden is highly dramatic. It represents in a physically understandable way what the fall from awareness meant. The temptation of power, then the nakedness of unawareness and the struggle to get back to the former state are all there, once one looks beyond the literal representation. Similarly, the story of Cain and Abel, although they also existed, is dramatized to highlight the duality of the unaware state.

As we have already seen, life on Earth was designed to help souls find their way back to their former state of full awareness. The process of evolutionary growth, which we have called the grand design, started through various forms of non-human life; and, at a certain stage the time was ripe, in a manner of speaking, for the creation of the human species with the capacity to exercise free will. The evolution of the human race could ideally be likened to the growth of a child through adolescence to adulthood (and wisdom). In the early stages (childhood) a lot of discipline (regulation) is necessary, even to ensure survival. Thus, the Old Testament shows the Father repeatedly instructing the child, even to the extent of handing down Commandments. The emphasis on love in the New Testament mirrors the expected growth in consciousness as the child reaches adulthood. Now he has the key to the door that is love; a simple, positive message.

You want to know about Sodom and Gomorrah, and the Flood.

The Biblical version is that the inhabitants of Sodom and Gomorrah had reached such a level of depravity that God decided to send two angels to warn them that they would be destroyed if they did not change their ways. Only one man, Lot, listened to the angels; and because nobody else heeded the warning, Lot agreed to take his family away to safety. As they left, he and his wife and two daughters were warned not to look backwards, but his poor wife, presumably overcome by curiosity, yielded to the temptation to look back and was immediately turned into a pillar of salt. Fire and brimstone destroyed Sodom and Gomorrah and all their inhabitants.

In the telling of the story, the moral took precedence over the facts. Sodom and Gomorrah existed. Though they were described as cities, they were only small communities or towns compared with what would be described as cities today. The biblical version clearly indicates that the "sin" of the inhabitants of Sodom and Gomorrah was homosexuality; it is stated that the male inhabitants came to Lot's house and tried to get the angels, who were male, to come out so that they could have "sex" with them. Lot is reported to have pleaded with them to take his two daughters instead (which doesn't say much for the value placed on women's status at the time). His offer was, apparently, not accepted, but the angels succeeded in getting Lot and his daughters safely away before the fire and brimstone descended.

So what did happen? If you substitute Abraham for God you have the key to the story, and, of course, Abraham was (is) God in the sense that every soul is. Many complaints had been made to Abraham, who was Lot's uncle and who was accepted as a type of patriarchal overlord of the region, about the behavior of the inhabitants of Sodom and Gomorrah. He yielded to pressure and sent two representatives (angels, as all souls) to warn them that he would destroy them and all their possessions if they didn't change their ways. They didn't listen and the representatives set fire to the towns while the people were sleeping. Lot's wife strenuously objected to leaving. She wept copiously (pillar of salt), lay on the ground and refused to move. She literally died of a broken heart.

The happening of Sodom and Gomorrah has been repeated many times over throughout the history of the world. "Righteous" people in the name of God have carried out countless acts of destruction. How many children and adults have been terrorized by being threatened with God's anger and eternal punishment (fire again) if they didn't behave themselves according to God's rules interpreted, of course, by God-fearing people!

In fairness to Abraham, one of the considerations influencing him, apart from righteousness, was that continuation or extension of the practices of the inhabitants of Sodom and Gomorrah would jeopardize the survival of the human race.

According to Genesis, and, indeed, historically, Noah lived long before Abraham. Noah is mostly remembered as the man who, with his family and selected animals, survived in a specially designed ark, the great flood which destroyed all other life on Earth. The biblical version, if taken literally, is a horrific story of a wrathful, unmerciful God inflicting destruction on the scale of a nuclear holocaust in modern times. But, of course, that couldn't have happened since such a God didn't and doesn't exist. What really happened was that there was a flood that was confined to the particular part of the world in which Noah lived. For the chroniclers of the Bible that was the entire world; in those days of restricted communication the extent of the world was very limited as far as those living in it were concerned. Noah had the foresight to be well prepared. The story is accurate within its own terms once the limits of the world within the knowledge and vision of the tellers are recognized. It doesn't take much of a leap of the imagination to ascribe such an apparently enormous disaster to a wrathful God, and to see Noah as specially singled out and favored by God. Even today, what are regarded as disasters, e.g., AIDS, are often described as, and believed to be, punishment by God for misbehavior. And it doesn't have to be a major disaster; plaintive cries such as, "What did I do wrong? Why am I being punished like this?" are commonplace responses to everyday happenings.

The Bible is really an account of the human experiment up to a certain stage, with all its struggles and traumas and coming to terms with its freedom of expression. It is not an objective account; all the contributors to it, to a greater or lesser extent, directed their efforts subjectively according to their own points of view, or the points of view which they deemed to be required of them. It is also (understandably) selective. For example, the real Jesus was different in many respects from the Jesus portrayed in the Gospels. One of the most striking things about Jesus was his sense of humor. The pietistic and somewhat punitive, albeit compassionate, representation of him in the Gospels emerged from the editing and re-editing processes and were in line with the thinking of an organization which was constantly extending its power base; love and humor are not seen as effective methods of control. In fairness to the chroniclers, most of the sentiments attributed to him were expressed by Jesus and the words used convey those sentiments accurately enough, although, of course, he said and did many things which are not recorded and which, if they had been, would have given a much more rounded picture of him. He was a compassionate, loving, humorous man, who was hot-tempered and often impatient, especially in his earlier years. He was much more relaxed in himself by the time he came to fulfill his public mission as Jesus. The last thing he wanted was to be put on a pedestal and adored. His aim was to bring people with him, not to set himself apart from them. If he were not so aware of the grand design he would have found it difficult to endure all the suffering that has been caused in his name. However, he realizes that he was a catalyst, a harbinger of changing consciousness, and he is happy about that.

If you look up John's Gospel you will see that Jesus is recorded as telling his disciples about a comforter/counselor who would be sent by the Father "to be with you for ever," "to teach you all things." He was, of course, talking about the grand design, the process by which souls from what I have categorized as the fourth stage of evolutionary growth act as guides or guardian angels for those souls who are still struggling along the path of increasing awareness.

There's nothing new, really, in what I'm communicating to you. I'm putting somewhat differently and from a new perspective what has been transmitted by many others through the centuries. An aspect of the Earth experience is that mystique, like dust, increases with the passage of time if it isn't cleared away.

Prophecy: No Big Deal

Trying to foretell the future is as old as time; that's an appropriate way of putting it since it's only in a framework of time that prophecy comes into its own.

Through the ages many seers and prophets have made many predictions, some accurate, some partly so, and some completely off the mark. In particular, there are various predictions about the last part of the present century that would seem to presage dire happenings, followed in some predictions by the end of the world and Judgment Day, and in others by a new age, perhaps a golden age.

Of course, in human terms every day there are dire happenings as there have been since life on Earth began. But the predictions generally foretell more cataclysmic events far beyond what is already happening.

How does prophecy occur? One common ground that prophets seem to have is that their prophecies come to them, or through them, from a higher source. Imagine life on Earth as a merry-go-round with a soul in spirit looking down on it. It sees what's happening at each stage of the round. For instance, in the case of a person getting on at a particular point, the soul looking down can see the pattern of events that are likely to unfold for that person while he stays on the round. It can also see what's happening at all stages on the round. It can see the past and future progression of the person on the round; what seems to be a prophecy to the person who is, say, at point X is really only a description of what's happening at point Y from the viewpoint of the soul looking down.

That's prophecy reduced to very simple terms in order to give you an understanding of how it works. There is nothing psychic or mystifying about it; think of the merry-go-round.

Generally speaking, all prophecy can do is outline a likely pattern of events. If people are working with their plans, then it is relatively easy to see how they will fit into the pattern. Even if they are not, it is still possible to predict how they will react to a given situation in line with the way they normally express themselves through their free will.

If you visualize life on Earth as a merry-go-round then you can see that what you call the past must also be the future. For instance, if you get on at point A and go on to points B, C, etc., when you reach point C, point B will be in your past. However, at some stage you may again get on at point A; then point B will be in your future. Thus do events and civilizations keep on repeating themselves. Souls change, their reaction to events change, and they progress in awareness through the experiencing of events which appear to be changing but are really repeating themselves, as in the natural order of things (seasons, grass, flowers, etc.).

Is all that clear enough? I hope you can see now why prophecy is no big deal. In the final analysis it can be reduced to two factors: one, astuteness of interpretation on the part of souls in spirit in the reading of patterns of behavior and fitting them into events; and two, clarity of communication between these souls and persons on Earth. In the second factor I include the capacity of persons on Earth to receive and interpret accurately what they receive.

Well, then, are all these catastrophes going to happen, as foretold, before the end of the present century? What does your reason tell you?

The acceleration of growth in technology in the present century has increased the possibilities of more devastating conflicts. Such conflicts have happened, are happening, and will continue to happen. However, there will be no cataclysmic happening, such as the end of the world, in this century nor, indeed, in any century. Ultimately, of course, life on Earth as you know it will cease but that will not happen until it no longer serves as a learning experience, and then it will be a gradual process of evolution, a natural process.

As I have said in an earlier session, the process of growth in awareness has also accelerated and will continue to do so. Revolutions in thinking are already taking place and in this sense it can be said that Earth is moving into a golden age. But there will be no such thing as separating the goats from the sheep. One of the big advantages of life on

Earth for growth purposes is that souls at different levels of awareness come into contact with each other with beneficial effects for those at the lower levels. It would be unthinkable that the grand design would exclude any soul, or group of souls, from the possibility of continuing benefit.

Prophecy: a Perception of Time

Why is there so much hit and miss about prophesy? Surely it is possible for a soul looking down on the merry-go-round to foresee that certain events will happen even allowing for the free will of the people involved since within the context of a *continuing* present these events are already happening? For instance, is the soul not able to see newspaper headlines as they will be?

The most important thing to be said is that it is not possible for any soul, no matter what its level of awareness, to predict with a one-hundred-percent degree of accuracy what's going to happen and when it's going to happen. This is, of course, because of free will. For instance, the only thing I can predict with certainty is that all souls must eventually get back to full awareness. I make that prediction because it is not possible that souls can exist indefinitely in a condition contrary to their nature, and also because the grand design is so comprehensive and flexible and its pattern of success is so well established that I cannot envisage failure for it even in respect of one soul. But I have no idea as to when my prediction will be fulfilled, except that there is a long time to go yet.

Suppose that I'm a soul looking down on the merry-go-round. I can see events as they are happening to people at a certain stage on the round and I can see that they are likely to repeat themselves for people coming up to that stage. But

53

because people may not continue to behave in accordance with their previous patterns, some of the events may not happen to them at all or they may happen in a different way or according to a different time scale. So my prediction may be totally wrong, or I may get it right in some respects, or I may get it right except for the timing. I cannot foresee newspaper headlines since I'm not in the habit of influencing newspaper editors or sub-editors as to what to put into the headlines!

A person's guides are much better able to predict that person's future than they are able to predict happenings, e.g., on a global scale, which are not directly connected with the person. The reason for this is that the person will have drawn up his life plan in conjunction with his guides. To the extent that he is staying with his plan his future is easier or harder to predict. (Incidentally, the sense of destiny which many people feel is accounted for by their inner knowledge of their plan; their plan is their destiny.)

Guides will never impose their will on another soul even if that soul is deviating from his plan. This is not true of souls at lower levels of awareness. Thus, a person may get a message from a spirit source that such and such is going to happen to him. He is then mentally conditioned to the event, and the soul in spirit, in its state of unawareness, will do all in its power to make it happen. The two influences working together will, in all probability, succeed, and in this way a prediction is fulfilled.

Nothing happens without purpose since everything that happens is given a purpose within the overall flexibility of the grand design. Life is a wonderfully evolving thing, not subject to the rigidity of pre-ordination. The only element of pre-ordination is each soul's life plan, and even that, as we have seen, can work within an unlimited framework of flexibility.

Of course, guides don't object to being questioned about the future. However, if the questioner shows a tendency towards being influenced in an obsessive way by the answers, the guides will more than likely give him increasingly contradictory answers in order to help him to rid himself of his obsessions. Trying to live in the future does nothing to help a person fulfill his purpose on Earth.

Souls in spirit are often not any wiser or more advanced than souls temporarily on Earth, but they are in a better position to see the overall picture of happenings on Earth and therefore to make more accurate predictions about the future. The more aware a soul is the less likely it is to make predictions if there is any risk that they may influence the exercise of free will. However, if that risk is not present, it will probably enjoy chancing its arm, or going out on a limb, if you prefer to put it that way!

PART II

The Stages of Evolutionary Growth

What do I do to occupy my time? Well, I'm free of all pressure to occupy myself in any way, and, as I said, time doesn't exist in this vibration.

The best thing I can do, probably, is to go through the different stages of evolutionary growth, as I promised in our first session.

The ninety-nine percent designed a pattern of evolution to help the one percent recover their lost awareness. This pattern may be broadly banded into seven stages with the seventh being that of full awareness. Within each of the other six stages there are many states of growth with movement through the different forms of non-human life representing progress in increasing awareness.

The first stage is the lowest stage of awareness. All non-integrated souls, parts of souls if you like, whether they are temporarily housed in physical bodies or are in spirit form, are at this stage.

The second stage includes the human state. Souls are once again integrated. They have not yet learned all the lessons that Earth existence or existence elsewhere can provide for them.

The third stage is one of appraisal or reappraisal where all the experiences the soul has acquired are evaluated. This is more a stage of reflection than of movement.

The fourth stage represents a considerable growth in awareness. Souls who have reached this stage do not, for instance, have any further lessons to learn from Earth existence. The guides are at this stage.

The fifth stage again includes much reflection and evaluation.

The sixth stage is one of great joy. The soul at last comes to know the full measure of what it had lost and has now found again. Before a soul leaves the sixth stage it will, of course, have regained full awareness so that it can enter the seventh stage.

Now I'll try to outline what happens at each of the stages.

The First Stage

How does a soul that has diffused itself into a million parts and lost all awareness of itself in the process begin to become aware? How can it help it to be expressed in physical existence as a million fleas? Insects survive by contact with other forms of life. Each one achieves some awareness even to a minute extent of something outside itself. For instance, a flea finds that it can feed off a human being! That little spark of awareness multiplied a million times may be enough to make it helpful for the soul to reincarnate in some other multiple physical species, such as mice. The idea is that with each incarnation awareness will increase. Initially the spur to awareness is purely the need for physical survival. Experiences eventually begin to raise the consciousness level until the soul reaches the point where it can see itself as an integrity.

The operation of free will has become suspended at this stage. Here the purpose of the grand design of evolutionary growth is to get the soul back to a state where it will once again be capable of exercising free will. As I have already said the grand design was brought into operation by the ninety-nine percent. No single facet of existence is accidental. Each creature has its own part to play towards one great purpose. Progress is controlled and guided by many souls. Part of the process of growth for souls who have become reintegrated is to help others less aware than themselves. Each soul, by agreement, is given specific tasks to do.

Respect for all creatures is an important feature of developing awareness. The knowledge of what each creature is will encourage respect.

I don't want to digress here into a discussion on eating habits but at the same time I can't leave the question hanging in the air. Non-human creatures kill each other to satisfy their hunger for food. Humans kill other creatures for food. (I know both human and non-human creatures kill each other for other reasons too, but these are directly related to awareness levels.) However, it's important to remember that only the physical bodies are involved. It's not a black and white question of right and wrong. Fishermen make their livelihood from catching and selling fish and many others are helped to survive physically by the fruits of their labors. Equally, many depend for sustenance on the proceeds from the raising of animals for eventual selling and slaughter as meat, as many do from the eating of meat. These practices don't necessarily hinder the process of growth; they may help it if done with respect.

The Second Stage

The soul has reached a state of awareness which makes it possible for it to achieve reintegration in one unit. It still has many lessons to learn, however, and these lessons have to be effective; that is, they must heighten the consciousness and awareness of the soul. The primary lesson is that it is one soul and that it has free will. It has many guides available to help it to see what other lessons it has to learn and to suggest options as to how they might be learned. One of the common options is incarnation in a human form in specially selected conditions, environmental and otherwise, which will throw up the types of experiences designed for the learning of particular lessons. Human beings did not physically evolve out of (other) animals although souls evolve through different types of physical non-human forms until they reach the human state, but each non-human state and the human state itself were specially designed by the ninety-nine percent (the Father) for the development of awareness.

The grand design of the Father, the ninety-nine percent, envisaged the materialization of a physical substance that would reflect in a material form the fluidity and infinity of love. Water was that substance. If you visualize water everywhere without any physical enclosure you will at least have a tangible image of infinity. Water came first and all other materializations evolved out of it. God (or love) created water and evolved out of it shapes and limits to contain it. Each creature, non-human and human, was specially designed out of water. That's the simple answer to all our beginnings in a physical environment. The process of natural procreation built into the design took care of the multiplication of each species.

If I may digress here again a little, I hope you will now see more clearly the significance of water. Physical life cannot exist without it, as you know. But symbolically, also, you can see its importance. Water is the essence of physical life as love is the essence of spiritual life.

Earth existence is only a part of the second stage. The soul has many options from which to choose, such as life on other planets. It may well choose to have a life on Earth followed by a life on another planet, or it may decide against either of these options. Earth is the best school of all from the point of view of shortening the journey to awareness. It places so many restrictions on the spirit that the only way of overcoming them is through increased awareness.

You are already well aware of Earth conditions. Spirit life generally, including life on other planets, is not subject to the same restrictions, and there is no birth or death. The soul is not housed in a body but retains its etheric form which is the form it has chosen in which to manifest itself as spirit. The soul is aware of its immortality, but it is confined to the vibration of its own level of consciousness, with the result that it does not come into direct contact with souls of higher awareness levels; and, thus, the process of attaining higher awareness can be a slow one. (Help is always available, of course, if requested.) Earth is a great leveler in that respect because the physical vibration is the same for all, so that souls at vastly different awareness levels come into frequent contact with each other with resultant benefit for at least some of them.

I referred above to the etheric form of the soul that is a shape on the lines of the physical form but without its material substance. Souls in spirit in the second stage of development appear to each other rather like humans do. The only difference is the heaviness of the Earth vibration. The souls also occupy themselves in much the same way as humans do but without the element of physical labor. For the sake of illustration let's take a day in the life of a spirit. He has no physical body, so he doesn't need sleep, so he doesn't wake up; he's already awake. However, he likes the idea of being in bed, so he's lying in bed. He also likes having breakfast so he decides what he wants and as he thinks of the different items of food they are there in front of him. He's in a house which corresponds to the type of house he imagines he would like. He feels he would like to listen to music for a while. He doesn't have to go to the trouble of playing a record or a tape or switching on anything, he can just think of whatever music he'd like to hear and he can hear it. Maybe he has some other soul or souls living with him if they are agreeable to do so. It might be his wife in a previous Earth existence, for example, if they are both in the same vibration. They may have a common interest in gardening, or listening to music, or theater, or reading, or walking, or whatever. All these things are available to them just by thinking about them. They may continue to share the experience of making love, if they want to. To sum up, our friend may spend his day and every day and night (I'm continuing to use the Earth time terminology . . . there are no days and nights in the spirit world) doing whatever he wants to do. He may want to go and look at what's happening to his relatives and friends on Earth, and even to try and influence them in any way he can. He's free to do this if he wants to unless the people on Earth ask their guides not to let any other influences get through to them.

So, if I may repeat myself to sum it all up, at the second stage of development life in spirit, which includes life on other planets, follows the same pattern as life on Earth except that birth and death and all the other physical happenings, such as accidents, illnesses, wealth, poverty, the labor involved in bringing a thought or an idea to materialization, only apply to Earth.

Why then would a soul with any degree of sanity choose an Earth life? And why do souls choose to remain earthbound after they have left their physical bodies? It's generally true that all souls who have been through an Earth experience are earthbound for a certain length of time. A mother who has left a husband and young children will continue to watch over them and try to help them. If they are constantly grieving for her she will find herself being pulled towards them and her suffering may be very intense because she cannot make her presence known to them. This is something that may perhaps be overlooked. The suffering of the people left behind is obvious but at least they can share it with each other. The mother knows that she could alleviate both her family's suffering and her own if only she could make contact with them. Sometimes she does succeed in meeting them while their bodies are asleep but they don't remember that in the morning, or if they do they dismiss it as a dream or as wishful thinking. The work being done by mediums in this connection can be very helpful because it can break the strong chain of grief. If the mother is able to establish contact with her family, a big burden is lifted from them and from her. They still have to face the vicissitudes of Earth life without her physical help but they know that she is there and that they will meet again which is a great consolation to them. All this while she can allow herself to take stock of herself in her new circumstances, and, in that process, she may begin to be aware of the design which makes suffering an unfortunately necessary but inevitably temporary part of life at her present stage of development. However, the mother may decide that she knows what's best for her husband and children, and for that reason she continues to stay around them day and night. That's one way of being earthbound. Not only will she interfere with her family's lives but she will also continue to hinder her own progress until she frees both them and herself from her obsession. All earthbound souls are slaves to obsessions.

On the face of it, there would appear to be no good reason why a soul should choose an Earth existence with all its difficulties over an apparently much easier spirit existence. However, after what may be a relatively short period of time, or a long time (there is no pressure), the soul begins to find itself coming up against its own prejudices or limitations which it has imposed on its thinking. For example, a person (for the sake of identification I'll call him Joseph) who followed a strictly orthodox religious tradition while on Earth passes on and expects to be judged by God and then assigned to heaven or hell or maybe purgatory. To his surprise he finds that he is much the same as he was when on Earth. He even has a body although it feels much lighter. He can see his relatives around his Earth body; it may take him some time to realize that it is his body and that he in fact "died." He may hover around the scene for some time observing the funeral arrangements, etc., but eventually he will become aware of others whom he knew on Earth calling to him or talking to him or simply looking at him. He doesn't hear things in the same way as he did on Earth. While the sounds are clear they seem to be in his head rather than external to him. The others appear to be as they were on Earth except that they look younger and more vigorous. Soon he is talking to them, as he would have done on Earth. They take him to one of their houses and the journey seems to be accomplished without any effort. They probably sit around and have tea or whatever he feels like having. He is, of course, perplexed. Can this be hell? Surely not. Is it heaven, perhaps? His friends tell him that it is and, as far as they are concerned, that's the truth. He asks them have they seen God and have they been judged. They reply, with some puzzlement, that they haven't but that maybe they haven't been here long enough yet. He asks can he still carry out his religious observances, and they answer "yes," that everything is just the same. The only thing that surprises them is that others who believed differently from them, heretically in their eyes, seem to be here too, except that, of course, they don't attend their religious services.

With the passage of time Joseph settles happily into a routine which suits his thinking. He has his friends, his religious practices, his hobbies. However, questions begin to niggle at him. Where is God? How come he hasn't been judged? How is it that others whom he regarded as sinners seem to have arrived in heaven too? Then one day, one of his friends tells him he's leaving. Joseph is mystified. What! Leaving heaven! How can one do that? Why? His friend explains to him that he has found out that a lot of his thinking was limited by his conditioning, that he has been living in too superficial a way, that he now wants to learn more and to progress further spiritually. He has decided that he will go back to Earth for another lifetime in order to undergo experiences and to learn certain lessons from them.

Joseph has now come face to face with a difficult situation. It looks as if what he believes is heaven isn't really heaven at all. And here was his friend talking about reincarnating! This was contrary to what he had been taught in his religion. Surely so many wise and learned churchmen couldn't be mistaken in their teaching? His friend understands his position fully; he has been through it all himself, and, he says that if Joseph asks God for guidance about these and other questions that will occur to him he'll be sure to get it; that's what he did.

Joseph's friend leaves and he slips back into his routine. But the niggle has now become more like a shout, and one day he decides to ask God for guidance as his friend had suggested. Immediately a soul that he cannot recollect having met before appears before him. He is friendly and helpful and he explains that he has come in answer to Joseph's request for guidance. He says that he will be available to Joseph for as long as he wants him, that he has only to send a mental request to him and he will come. He explains to Joseph that he (Joseph) has reached a certain stage in spiritual development but that he has many other things to learn. With the help of visual images he takes him through many of his previous experiences, including Earth lives, and shows him that before he reincarnated he set out for himself the purpose of each life. Joseph sees where he succeeded and where he failed. His guide explains to him that there are many things outside of his (Joseph's) perception at present and that he will reach understanding and awareness of them only by freeing himself from the limitations that he imposed on himself. This in turn could best be done either through a further series of Earth experiences with the help of a physical body, or by remaining in the spirit world and continuing to learn there. He would be likely to make faster but probably more painful progress by opting for another Earth life and the choice is entirely up to him. If he chooses to be reincarnated he would be helped in the choice of parents and environment and the whole process could be arranged by agreement between the prospective parents and himself; or, alternatively, he could make his own choice of environment and take "potluck" on the parents if he wanted to reincarnate more quickly than would be possible under the other type of arrangement. Also, if he chooses to be reincarnated he could, if he wished, ask for a soul or souls who had reached an advanced stage of awareness to be assigned to him as a guide or guides and the guide or guides will work with him before his reincarnation and guide him insofar as he allows them to during his Earth life. On the other hand, if he chooses to stay in the spirit world, he could attend regular sessions with others who were at a like stage of development as himself and who had also asked for guidance where guides would be available to help them grow in awareness. Or he could try another environment, still in spirit form, which would be specially selected for him.

Here it is necessary to digress for a moment to explain that when I talk about a soul being someplace in the spirit world it is not occupying space in the same way as humans do. In fact, the spirit world is all around you; souls continue to live their lives in circumstances that very often seem to be the same as Earth circumstances, but they are not anywhere in particular. The place is the mind, if you like, or in the mind, or perhaps, more accurately, in the awareness. So spirit life can simulate the conditions of Earth or of another planet until ultimately no simulation is needed; but Earth is the only planet in which there is materialization. The only significance in talking about life on another planet is that a soul or souls can be isolated for a specific purpose in a particular type of environment which is dissimilar to the environment with which they had become familiar; other planets are reflections of such types of environment. It is not outside the bounds of possibility that at some stage there will be physical or material existence on other planets such as there is on Earth. That depends on whether the Earth experiment achieves its purpose without stretching the boundaries of pain to an extent that would be unendurable for human beings.

To return briefly to Joseph: he decides that he will opt for the unfamiliar, the other environment. The particular one chosen for him is the planet Uranus. There is apparently no other life around him. He is, of course, still in spirit form so that he doesn't need any physical sustenance. As far as he is concerned he's on his own. For as long as he can remember he has relied on tradition and ritual and the security of conformity in the living of his life. Now he has none of these things. The hope is that when he eventually realizes that all his props are now no use to him he will begin to turn inwards and try to come to know himself. He may find the experience too much for him; if so, he can ask to be returned to his previous situation. On the other hand, if he finds himself strengthened by the experience he may be ready to open his mind to other ideas and to move on to the third stage.

The abiding impression I want to leave with you of the second stage is that it all happens as part of the Father's grand design of growth in awareness. The fact that part of the experience takes place on Earth is immaterial. You are spirit and you are you whether or not you are temporarily housed in a physical body.

The Third Stage

This, as I said, is a stage of re-evaluation and reflection. From now on the question of place doesn't arise because there is no materialization. However, if you want to have some image of place, you can imagine weightless beings with all the freedom and space of air and more besides.

The soul has probably had many experiences on Earth and also purely as spirit. It is now open-minded enough to be able to go through them all in detail to see where they were all leading and to assess its present position.

At this stage there is no longer any need for souls to identify themselves in terms of sex. The division of the human race into male and female was desirable primarily for procreation purposes but it also served as a useful means for a soul to acquire varied and contrasting experiences through male and female lives. The etheric body retains its sexual characteristics, but that body has served its purpose after the second stage and it is discarded on entry into the third stage.

I think that the easiest way to illustrate how the transition from second to third stage takes place and what happens then is to continue with the story of Joseph. He has been put into an isolated situation without any of the props to which he had become accustomed. There's nothing he can do but think. The loneliness is difficult at first and many times he's on the point of asking to be taken back to his earlier situation (which he had been assured could be done through a mental request to his guide). However, he perseveres and eventually he begins to analyze his thinking on various issues. He finds that he has been praying to God for as long as he can remember but that he has no concept of God beyond that of an all-powerful, all-merciful, all-just, but hazy figure. There is a strong element of fear built into his idea of God. He accepted without question all that he was taught about right and wrong, sin and forgiveness of sin, reward and punishment. Events since his last physical death initially confirmed him in his beliefs but later threw doubt on at least some of them. When on Earth, he thought of heaven as being with God, but what he would be doing he had no idea. He thought of hell as a place of eternal fire but beyond feeling that he didn't want to end up there he hadn't any image of it. Later, he thought he was in heaven, although it didn't conform to his earthly image of it, vague as that was. Then, later still, he found that it wasn't really heaven and that he needed to make further progress in spiritual development.

So the long lonely days pass. Then one day he hears a voice saying clearly to him, "You are God." Horrified, he puts the thought away from him as being unutterably blasphemous. But a little later the voice repeats its message and it keeps on repeating it at intervals for many days with the effect that, while Joseph still cannot accept it, he cannot avoid thinking about it. Then the message changes to "And so is every soul" which introduces a new dimension and makes the idea somewhat more acceptable to him. This is a major step forward in his growth of awareness. Once the idea takes hold he sees himself and every other soul in a completely new light. He begins to realize his own importance as a soul and also that every other soul without exception is equally important. Once he has fully accepted his place in spirit he is ready for the third stage.

The voice was that of Joseph's guide (who, by agreement between them, was continuing to help Joseph). If the guide had given the second message first, Joseph would probably have rejected it. The impact of the first message was so great that, by comparison, it was a great relief to get the second one, and, of course, it was all the more acceptable for that. The method used to try to raise Joseph's awareness was particularly suited to his state of isolation; if he went around saying that he was God there was nobody to accuse him of megalomania or some other form of lunacy. His guide was able to judge Joseph's readiness to accept the messages. It's one thing to give a message and another to accept it; which is the reason why there's so much trauma attached to the journey back to full awareness.

There's no dramatic business of stepping over the threshold from one stage to another. All that happens is that the state of awareness changes. The guides who make arrangements for further development know this.

Because of the change in his state of awareness Joseph finds that he is no longer in isolation. His first impression is of being surrounded by light. He is not conscious of being anywhere in particular; it's not like a room or a house or any enclosure. He's very comfortable but he doesn't seem to be standing up, sitting down, or lying down. Now he becomes aware that the light is really a number of separate shapes. As he becomes more accustomed to his surroundings he sees that the shapes are beings apparently clothed in robes with features similar to those of humans.

I said that the etheric body that is used in the non-human states of the second stage is discarded on entry into the third stage. The etheric body is a reproduction in nonmaterial form of the last physical body used by the soul, or if the soul never incarnated in a physical body it represents its choice of manifestation. At the third stage, the appearance, or manifestation, represents the individual characteristics of the soul, or, more accurately, the individual being that the soul is. The appearance literally mirrors the soul and nothing is hidden. I'll be going into this in more detail later.

Joseph finds that he doesn't have to say anything; that thoughts seem to be projected towards him by the other beings and that they seem to be picking up his thoughts. There's a marvelous feeling of harmony all around him and within him.

One of the beings communicates to Joseph that, if he wishes, he will guide him through this particular stage. Joseph agrees. He finds himself alone with his guide who takes him through his complete history as a soul. This is a comprehensive in-depth analysis and there is no selectivity involved as there was when Joseph had previous Earth experiences shown to him at the second stage. There's nothing judgmental about the analysis; it's an objective appraisal and Joseph is now able to look at everything in a detached and dispassionate way. He sees the whole process by which he lost his awareness and the painful journey back to where he now is. Nothing, no matter how apparently small or insignificant, is ignored. He sees that he sank to the lowest levels of degradation, that some of his thoughts and actions could only be described as horrible, that he went through states of pomposity and cruelty and hypocrisy. He also went through states of deprivation and extreme hardship, and he had many thoughts and performed many acts of kindness and beauty. He observes the pattern of the grand design and how time and time again it is obstructed by his unawareness in the use of his free will, but also how time and time again it adjusts itself to his changing needs.

The analysis or evaluation takes a long time as Joseph is of a slow and thorough disposition. The time taken doesn't matter. What's important is that he shouldn't move from any happening without thoroughly grasping its meaning. His evaluation finishes when his acceptance of who and what he is and his place in God is total. In other words, that it's not just an intellectual acceptance but also a feeling one; that he knows it within and with his whole being.

At the end he's filled with wonder at the way in which the design worked in his case, and with joy that no soul can be overlooked in its operation. He's filled with an indescribably beautiful feeling of oneness with God, although some sadness still remains that he should have separated himself from that feeling for so long and that so many others still don't remember and experience that feeling.

The Fourth Stage

The soul has now reached a full acceptance of its place in God and a full appreciation and understanding of all its experiences since it began its fall from awareness and of how these experiences fitted into the grand design.

Some souls who have reached the fourth stage choose to go back to Earth to try to help others. They themselves have no longer any lessons to learn from the Earth experience. At the same time by taking on a physical body and going through the states of childhood and adolescence with all the conditioning involved in that process, they obscure their awareness and sometimes they may reach a relatively late stage in their Earth lives before the veil of obscurity is lifted. But they always know that they have a particular purpose in life and sooner or later they find it. This purpose is usually a common one for a number of souls only one of whom will reincarnate. The others will act as his guides. The number of such souls on the Earth plane has increased considerably in recent years and is now approximately one million. Much care has been exercised in the choice of location(s) for their physical existence. They usually operate quietly and unobtrusively and do not seek positions of prominence in the communities in which they live. However, opportunities are created through which their wisdom, including, of course, the wisdom of their guides, is imparted to others who are ready to receive it or even a small part of it.

Souls at the fourth stage also operate as guides to all other souls in lower vibrations who have asked for guides. One human being may have a number of guides, so obviously the guides occupy themselves in other ways also, while they are, of course, always available to help the person being guided.

Perhaps it would be helpful if I first outlined the system by which guidance works and then went on to say something about the other ways in which souls at the fourth stage occupy themselves.

A soul decides to reincarnate. His particular purpose is, say, to learn the virtue of tolerance. He accordingly chooses an environment in which he will meet many different types of people with strongly contrasting opinions. His guide or guides who are working with him in spirit advise him that it would be desirable for him to have more than one guide helping him since he will be faced with a variety of situations and it would be helpful to have guides with him who had themselves coped with similar situations successfully. He accepts the advice. Through a form of mental communication rather like sending messages by computer his guide gets into immediate contact with some souls who have mastered the particular conditions. They all meet and it is decided between them that four of them will act as guides to the reincarnating soul. The guide or guides who have been working with him may or may not be part of the group of guides who will be helping him in his Earth existence.

Now the five of them, the four guides and the reincarnating soul, get together. The Earth environment has already been chosen. The prospective parents have to be selected. Usually souls who have been through Earth experiences together already choose to reincarnate in groups. Sometimes the parents in a previous existence become the children in another, or brothers and sisters become parents and children, or souls who have been married to each other choose to reincarnate in similar relationships or with roles reversed. Sometimes a soul may wish to have a totally new set of Earth relationships although this doesn't happen very often and is usually not successful.

At this stage, ideally, both the prospective parents and child or children are still all in spirit. If this is so they can come together with all their guides and share their plans for their Earth existence. It will be the guides' function to help the reincarnating souls accomplish what they planned to do.

The decision has been made, the parents and environment selected, the whole group with their guides, including any other souls who may choose to be born to the same parents and their guides, have had preparatory sessions together. The prospective parents move on to Earth; the prospective children continue to live in spirit until their time to be born comes.

Now the physical body is being prepared within the mother's womb. The soul and his guides work on the body to shape it to the soul's requirements for his particular purpose on Earth. While the physical body is in the mother's womb, the soul does not normally stay in it until very close to the time of birth. Sometimes it does not stay in it during the process of birth and may even decide that the body doesn't suit its purpose, which accounts for stillborn births. The pressure of the physical confines takes away most of the consciousness of what has gone before although some of it remains with the growing child until it is usually removed by conditioning. This is, of course, part of the grand design; it represents a real growth in awareness if the soul can reach even some of its consciousness of what it is while subject to the physical limitations of Earth existence.

If there is more than one guide each will usually have taken responsibility for certain aspects of the soul's development. They work in harmony and each knows automatically what the other is doing. There's always one of them watching over their human trust who normally doesn't remember anything about them or his arrangement with them. Again this is deliberate. If during his human existence he can reach an acceptance of his guides once he is informed about them, and opportunities will be provided for him to be so informed if his guides consider that he has reached a state of development where this would be helpful for him, then he is obviously making good spiritual progress. It's easy to accept a guide if you see him beside you or opposite you; it's not so easy if you don't and if you're subject to the constraints of human respect and all that goes with it.

Most guides still operate within a climate of ignorance of their existence on the part of the human beings whom they have agreed to help. If the human is living a positive life, for instance, if he generally looks on the bright side of things and is at peace with himself, it is much easier for the guides to help him. They can do this by way of suggestion—how often do you hear people saying, "The thought just came to me out of the blue" or "I just felt I had to go there"—or by direct guidance while the body is asleep. How many times do people go to bed with a problem and wake up with a solution to it without any memory of how they arrived at the solution? During a person's waking hours the guides communicate generally through the pituitary and pineal glands. They're a bit like prompters off-stage during a play. If an actor gets too fussed or excited or worried he won't be able to pick up a prompt; if he stays calm and relaxed he will.

What are the guides doing when they're off duty(!) from their guidance work? Sometimes they're helping more than one person. They're not necessarily doing developmental things all the time. One of the great things about having reached the fourth stage is that one can enjoy being relaxed without feeling any sense of guilt or reservation about it. Just being and enjoying the feeling is a great pleasure. Get-togethers about the progress of the grand design, philosophical discussions, creative projects, communication with others on what might be called a social level are some of the ways in which souls at the fourth stage occupy them-selves. All the souls at this stage still in spirit do not act as guides. A creative project may, for example, take the form of a literary exercise or a scientific experiment. All such proj-ects are geared towards helping other souls reach the fourth stage. Much inspirational writing, including poetry, plays, novels, philosophical treatises, has resulted from such cre-ative projects.

Souls who are acting as guides also act as channels for other souls from higher and lower vibrations to get through to human beings. It is, of course, possible for souls at the second stage who are in spirit to get through directly to humans, and many do; but the guides will gladly act as chan-nels if they are asked to do so. Normally a soul from a higher vibration than the fourth will not seek to get through to a human and will send any message he may have through the guides. When a soul from a higher vibration wishes to get through directly to a human he will only do so by arrange-ment with the guides and the human concerned.

It is sometimes said that guides, because they are in a higher vibration, cannot prevent souls from a lower vibra-tion getting through to humans due to the fact that the lower vibration is closer to Earth. That is not so. Guides have no difficulty getting through to humans if the latter do not put up barriers against them. The very fact that the guides' vibration is higher makes it more powerful. Once the guides are asked not to let any other spirit through except by arrangement with the human being concerned, they regulate the opening and closing of the centers by which communication is effected and no other soul can open the centers, except the human himself.

A soul can, of course, stay at the fourth stage for as long as it wishes. Some souls have decided that they will stay at that stage until all other souls have caught up with them. It's entirely a matter of free will; there's no pressure either way. It's hardly necessary to say that by moving on to the higher stages a soul will still be able to help others. Help is flowing from the Father always as the source of the grand design of help.

The Fifth Stage

The second and fourth stages involve a lot of activity. The fifth is rather like the third in the sense that it is again a stage mainly of reflection and re-evaluation.

Movement from the second stage through the third into the fourth is the biggest transition in the process of development. It is very difficult for a soul to accept, in the fullest possible sense of the word "accept," that it is really a part of God with all that that means; once it has reached the state of full acceptance the rest is much easier. It's not possible to move from the second stage through the third to the fourth without such acceptance in every part of the soul's being. Since the acceptance is already there at the fourth stage, there's no barrier against movement from the fourth stage to the fifth except the personal wish of the soul. As I have already said, many souls have chosen to remain at the fourth stage until all others have reached that stage; and it is generally with some reluctance that any soul moves from the fourth stage because there the concept of what happens to one happens to all becomes very much a reality and there is a deep concern that every soul should be given every possible help to reach the level of awareness that the souls at the fourth stage have regained. Normally a soul will not move from the fourth stage until it knows that it will be able to help others at least as effectively as it could from the fourth stage.

In outlining the different stages I have tried to give as simple a picture as possible of each, and in simplifying I have, of course, excluded a lot of detail. Insofar as the fifth, sixth and seventh stages are concerned the outline will have to be brief since I can find no way of giving a full picture which would be within the comprehension of any soul limited by the physical constraints of physical existence on Earth.

A soul who moves on to the fifth stage and beyond will not normally reincarnate in a physical body. It is, of course, possible for it to do so but it is not part of the grand design that it should. However, the design is continually flexible in its operation.

The type of re-evaluation that takes place at the fifth stage is of a global nature. The soul is already aware of and accepts its place in God, and has completed its personal re-evaluation at the third stage. Now with other souls at a similar stage of development it becomes aware of the whole sweep of the grand design and it is given an opportunity to study it in all its aspects. It can literally see love infusing all life.

The Sixth and Seventh Stages

Having completed the re-evaluation at the fifth stage, the soul is automatically at the sixth stage. The sixth stage is really a broadening out of the fourth. There's a big change in the state of being which I can't describe; it's a matter of feeling which in any case I wouldn't try to describe as it's one of the marvelous experiences in store for every soul on the way back to awareness. Once the broadening out is achieved the soul is at the seventh stage.

Souls at these stages oversee the grand design. Specific responsibilities are taken on by agreement.

My particular function or area of responsibility is to transmit to humans of what I have in such a way as to help them to raise their level of awareness. I cannot do this without a human agency. Lest you think that you are merely a channel, that's not so; you are a channel, of course, but I'm only giving you the thoughts not the words. If you didn't have the words to express my thoughts I wouldn't be able to communicate at all in the human sphere. Given your acceptance, my task is easy. But you had first to accept that it wasn't your imagination playing tricks on you, and second to make the commitment to put my thoughts on paper and to share them with others, with the attendant risk of forfeiting your carefully nurtured image of conformity, or at least inconspicuousness.

Here I'd like to take up a point about the contrast between the one percent who will have worked their way back to full awareness and the ninety-nine percent who never lost any of their awareness. Could it be argued that the one percent will then be more aware than the ninety-nine percent since the one percent will have been through so many experiences and so much suffering and the ninety-nine percent won't? Full awareness is full awareness and there can be nothing higher than that. An aspect of full awareness is unity; what happens to one happens to all. In a very real sense all the suffering experienced by the one percent was and is also experienced by the ninety-nine percent. It could, as a counter argument, be said that the suffering experienced by the ninety-nine percent individually is greater than that experienced by any one of the one percent since each soul part of the ninety-nine percent feels the suffering of all whereas each soul part of the one percent usually only feels his own. However, the only answer is that full awareness is the ultimate equality.

The grand design was prepared and implemented by the ninety-nine percent who have always been at the seventh stage. Energy is flowing from them at all times to all souls at the different stages. Many souls unfortunately block themselves off from the energy by their own anxieties and guilts and tensions. The seventh stage is heaven if you like to call it that.

Since the fall from awareness first happened and during all the traumatic times in the meantime much attention has been given by the Father (the ninety-nine percent) to the development and implementation of the grand design. You have heard it said that everything comes from the Father; that is literally true. For purposes of illustration it is helpful to think of the stages in vertical terms with energy flowing constantly from the top right down through all the souls at every stage with no chance of even one soul being overlooked in any way.

But what's the seventh stage of heaven really like? Well, for a start, try to imagine a state of being in which there's no pressure of any kind to do anything, to be anything other than yourself, knowing that every other soul sees you and loves you as you are without pretense and that you do likewise with them. It's difficult for a soul subject to the limitations of human existence to conceive of unlimited freedom of being. That's what life at the seventh stage is. It's not possible to do justice to it with words. It's a feeling that has to be experienced.

I don't want to leave you with the impression that what you're striving towards is a sort of an ultimate nirvana where nothing happens and where the idea of every soul being so happy all the time sounds boring in terms of eternity. Perhaps the best thing I can do is to outline how I occupy myself. I will first give brief details of my life history to try to summarize on the basis of one soul's experience what I have given you about the various stages.

As a slight digression may I say that I chose to categorize the stages into seven with the first being the lowest and the seventh the highest because I want to show the process of development in an orderly and simple way from the ground up, as it were. But, of course, it doesn't matter whether you choose to call the seventh the first or indeed categorize the stages in a totally different way. All that matters is that you should understand that there is a planned evolutionary progression and that things don't happen by chance.

As I told you, I was one of the one percent. I was attracted by the idea of having power over others and once I got used to the experience of having power, I wanted more and more of it. The more I gained power the less respect I had for those who allowed me to have that power. I was one of the instigators of the multiplication of the one percent into parts and, of course, I did it myself. Out of myself I created two parts which seemed to be exact reproductions of me. Everything was fine for a while until I found that I couldn't control the parts. They wanted to reproduce themselves, and did, and so it went. With each reproduction I was diminished and eventually I reached the stage where I was no longer aware of anything. The nearest equivalent in physical terms is a coma, or an extreme state of drunkenness, or of being drugged. I was brought back through various forms of insect and animal life to the stage which I have described as the second stage, where I became aware of myself as a soul. I won't bore you with the details of my human existences. There were 112 of them and through many of them my old obsession with power appeared again and again and was, I regret to say, often satisfied. Fortunately for me, my guides, many different guides, helped me grow until eventually, about 2,000 years ago, I moved into the third and, shortly afterwards, the fourth stages. From the fourth stage I reincarnated five times during the next 1,500 years. Then I decided that it was time for me to move on to the fifth and sixth stages. Through the love of the Father I have now regained my full awareness and am back where I started, having, alas, contributed in no small way to the cosmic pool of suffering.

Incidentally, I would like to emphasize that the fact that I have regained my former status doesn't confer any unusual distinction on me. Most are, and all must be, as I am. If I can get there, anybody can, and I mean that most sincerely.

At present, of course, I'm occupied to a certain extent in transmitting these thoughts to you, and, as I said, I'm always available for that purpose. I'm in constant communication with your guides and with others about many things including the overall development of the grand design. Here souls meet and communicate with each other on a basis of friendship and love, but that doesn't preclude any soul from having particular friends. I have a number of special friends. We often engage in creative projects that are our equivalents of poetry, plays, novels, painting, or music. That's all still possible at the ultimate stage and in a much more satisfying way than at any other stage. We are no longer searching for meaning in life, of course, but we are expressing its beauty and many-faceted nature. I happen to be particularly interested in literary type activities but there's room for every type of interest. There's no sexual identification so there's no such thing as the resurrection of the physical body; but there is communion between souls in a way that can never be achieved through sexual intercourse. I can see my friends any time I like or I can be alone. If my friends don't want to see me, that's fine. There's never any misunderstanding of any kind. There are no exclusive clubs or groups, and no inequalities even to the slightest extent. That doesn't mean that we don't make fun at each other's expense. Each of us has his own individual personality that gives an endless variety to life and at the same time is a constant source of humor. We don't become totally transformed beings when we get back to the seventh stage; we mature, in a manner of speaking, and realize our full potential, and are free of all pressures. Even though you've forgotten the details, you and every other human being and every soul with any awareness know that there's an ultimate happiness waiting for you if you can but find it. The only trouble is that you tend to seek it everywhere but within yourselves which is the only place it can be found in a coming home to the full awareness of your place in God.

Free Will

Free will is at one and the same time an integral and most precious attribute of spirit, and the main obstacle to the achievement by the individual soul of full awareness of itself.

The nature of God (or love) is such that there can never be any question of imposition of will upon another soul by a soul who has reached self-awareness.

When expression evolved out of God into individual parts each part retained the full freedom of spirit that it always had. There was no such thing as reporting back to some superior being looking for permission to do this or that or the other; it was completely free to express itself in any way it chose. This is still the position and will always continue to be so; it cannot be otherwise.

I have already said that all must eventually return to a state of full awareness. This sounds more like predestination than free will. It is predestination in the sense, but only in the sense, that love cannot negate itself or any part of itself. A soul cannot be other than what it is, a spirit being, part of God, but it is entirely free to operate in any way it chooses. Free will is a matter of operation, not of being.

Take an example of a man who has a decision to make. He can choose one of a number of different options. The choice he makes may affect the way he lives his life and color his thinking but he is still basically the same person. That's the way free will operates. The soul, the essential being, remains unchanged, but its awareness level is affected by every act of free will.

If a soul, by an accumulation of acts of free will, reaches a certain level of awareness and decides, again by an act of free will, that it will remain at that level forever, how can I reconcile that with my statement that all must eventually return to a state of full awareness? The soul is, of course, free to make that decision and it remains at the level of awareness that it has chosen until it opts to move out of it. In practice, of course, no soul exists in isolation from all others. Sooner or later a decision to move is inevitable. The influence of love within the soul, the essence of its being, will continue to throw up experiences and guidance that will eventually help it to raise its level of awareness. The length of time this takes will be a result of the operation of the soul's free will in making its choices or decisions.

Have I made myself clear? The soul *is;* it *has* free will. I hope you can understand the distinction.

Respect for each soul's free will is an essential ingredient of spiritual development. Imposition or attempted imposition of will by one person on another, or by a group of people, on a person or people is a common feature of human existence and is one of the reasons why life on Earth is such a valuable learning experience from the spiritual point of view. Obvious examples are: wars, physical force, threats, torture, laws, religious obligations, supervisory control, armies, police, courts, politicians, civil servants, parents, teachers, religious leaders. The less obvious ones may be more interesting, such as: persuasion, hinting, pleading, feigning illness or incapacity of some kind, playing on illness or incapacity, nagging, conferring or withholding of sexual favors, acting the martyr, praying for somebody without his consent, letting him know about the prayers, using any form of mind control without the agreement of the person concerned, tradition, conformity, outward show, shame, withdrawal, sulkiness, boredom, sincere belief in certain codes of behavior or religious practices, perception of duty, skill, experience, sincere desire to help, faith, conviction that one knows what's best for another, lying, selectivity in argument or imparting information, reward, disciplinary measures, promises, creation of expectations, mystery, uncertainty, dependence, possessiveness, fear of not being accepted, insecurity, times of crisis.

Suppose a child decides that he would like to run over a cliff. The father sees that the child will be killed or badly injured if he doesn't intervene. So he stops him; an apparently clear-cut case of the father imposing his will on that of the child.

I said at the beginning of this session that the nature of God (or love) is such that there can never be any question of imposition of will by a soul who has reached self-awareness upon another soul. Where does that leave the father in the example given above? The child is not in a position to exercise choice. As he is a soul spiritually equal to his parents, he has chosen to place himself in his physical environment for a brief period of time under their care, with their agreement of course. The child, as spirit, would not be damaged by running over the cliff, but his physical body would. In his present state he is not aware of this. By his own choice, an act of free will, he has given his parents the right to exercise his free will on his behalf until he has become sufficiently aware of physical conditions to do it for himself.

Take another example. You are walking by a river and you see a woman about to throw herself into a particularly deep spot apparently with the intention of committing suicide. Do you stop her? If you do, aren't you showing disrespect for her free will? The answers here are "no," if you have reached a state of full awareness; and "yes." Remember that the woman is an indestructible spirit. By her act of physical destruction of her body she may well create a condition for herself which will ultimately help her to raise her awareness level. You are not likely to do her any favor in the long run by interfering, hard as that may be to accept if viewed from a physical or limited spiritual perspective.

You want to know what would be the position in the first example if the adult on the scene were not a parent of the child? The same. The adult would be in the place of the parent. The difference between the two examples is that in the first the child is not aware of what he's doing, in the second the woman is. If, on the way down to the water, or when she is in the water, the woman cries out for help, the picture is changed. She has now exercised her free will in a different direction. If you save her physically in that situation the effect on her awareness is likely to be far better than if you save her against her will before she jumps.

What about the position of parents insofar as the practice of religion by a child is concerned? The parents sincerely believe that it is in the best interests of the child to have the support of religious belief and religious practice, but the child finds it all too boring for words and will only practice under duress. The parents hope that habit will eventually create interest. This is, of course, a common situation and is an example of lack of respect for free will. Of what possible spiritual benefit can it be to anybody, child or adult, to be forced to take part physically in a ritual that has no meaning for him? This type of situation has caused more spiritual stagnation than any other.

If you feel you have found something in the spiritual field that has brought great joy to you, you naturally want to share it with everybody. How you share is the biggest test you will ever have of your growing awareness. If you are really aware, you will never seek to impose your beliefs in any way, either directly or indirectly, nor will you ever seek to convince others of the rightness or truth of those beliefs. The best you can do, and believe me it is the very best, is to make people aware of your beliefs in the most unobtrusive possible way when suitable opportunities, such as expressions of interest, present themselves.

In conclusion, I must apply what I have said to these sessions. With your agreement and cooperation they are being presented in written form so that people will be free to read them or not as they think fit. Acceptance of some or all or none of what's in the sessions is entirely an exercise of free will on the part of the reader. Whether you put an exclamation mark at the end of the last sentence is entirely an exercise of free will on your part!

Free Will in the Grand Design

I have talked about free will and what a key element it is in the nature of soul. I also said that nothing happens by accident. I can see that there is still some confusion in your mind about a possible contradiction between those two statements.

Once a soul evolves into the second stage its free will is again operative. This means that it has freedom of choice in all circumstances. For example, it chooses to reincarnate. Before doing so, it plans, with the help of guides if it so wishes, the course of its life on Earth, and it agrees with its guides—if it has chosen to have guides—that they will help it to follow that course. On Earth it has forgotten, at least on the surface, both the plan and the guides, but it still has free will.

Let's suppose that as part of its plan a soul has chosen to become a priest and take a vow of celibacy for the primary purpose of overcoming an obsession with sex. (Here I must remind you that all obsessions are of the mind and therefore carried through into spirit if they are not overcome during a lifetime on Earth.) During his early life on Earth his environmental conditions as well as his own inner knowledge of his plan and the efforts of his guides steer him in the direction of the priesthood. Yet his obsession is still there, and eventually he chooses to renounce the idea of becoming a priest. By an act of free will he has now reached a position where he has deviated from his life plan.

The important thing to remember, however, is that becoming a priest was only the means by which he had hoped to overcome his obsession. Now the flexibility of the grand design and its immediate agents, his guides, comes into operation. The guides continually engineer situations that will serve as learning experiences for him. They never lose sight of his main purpose on Earth which is to free himself from his obsession even though he himself may continue to indulge the obsession by his own acts of free will.

But suppose he marries and has children; in view of the fact that his plan was to become a priest there was surely no agreement made in spirit with other souls about marriage and children. In a case like this it is likely that the woman who agrees to marry him is also acting contrary to her life plan. The children who are born to them will have decided to avail themselves of an unscheduled opportunity to reincarnate rather than wait for the usual arrangements to be made for them. Even given the rather non-ideal circumstances of their reincarnation, however, the children will also have decided on their own life plan with, of course, the help of guides if so desired.

Generally speaking, people get married and children are born to them in accordance with arrangements made in spirit. The exceptions are rare. Obviously many marriages are unstable even from a very early stage. Nonetheless, it is likely that they are the fulfillment of prearranged plans. Divorces and remarriages are also likely to have been planned in advance. They are all learning experiences.

Marriage and children are obviously central issues in the lives of many people on Earth. Work is another. As a general rule, each soul, prior to reincarnation, chooses, with the help of its guides, the pattern of its entire working life on Earth. One of the functions of the guides is to help the soul now in a physical body to follow that pattern. Because of free will there are deviations from the pattern in many cases. By and large, these are only minor deviations and it is true as a generalization to say that each and every soul on Earth is in the best place and in the best work (or non-work) environment for it to fulfill its life purpose. It is, broadly speaking, relatively easy for guides to arrange what I might categorize as environmental or situational conditions such as work or marriage. The real difficulty is in helping souls to help themselves to benefit from the experiences that they themselves have chosen.

I must emphasize that in making their arrangements the guides are not in any way controlling or seeking to control a person's will. They are merely helping him to live his life under the conditions chosen by him prior to his birth. If, during his life on Earth, a person's choice of action conflicts with his plan, his guides will not seek to influence his decision but will instead seek to put opportunities in his way which will help him to achieve his life purpose even if he chooses to deviate from his plan.

I would like to make two points in support of my statement that nothing happens by accident or, perhaps put more clearly, that nothing that happens is an accident. First, every action involves an expression of choice, of free will. Second, even if an action is in conflict with a chosen plan, it still serves as a means of furthering a soul's life purpose due to the flexibility of the grand design in using each action, no matter how negative it may seem to be, as the basis of an opportunity to raise awareness.

The word accident is commonly used in today's world in connection with car crashes. Suppose a man leaves his home and drives with the utmost care on his usual route to work. He leaves his home at exactly the same time each morning, travels at the same speed and on the same route. He follows this pattern without incident for many years. Then one morning another car crashes into his. He is entirely blameless in so far as the crash is concerned; nevertheless he is severely injured.

How can my statement that nothing happens by accident be reconciled with that incident?

The man was in his car on the road by his own choice, an act of free will on his part. This was as true on the morning of the crash as it was on every other morning. It was entirely his own choice that he should follow a particular pattern of operation consistently each morning. It may well have been part of his plan that he should have been involved in the crash; for instance, as a means of compelling him to question his values and attitudes. In any event, whether it was or it wasn't part of his plan, his guides will use it to help him achieve the purpose for which he reincarnated.

It is obviously much easier for human beings if they can stay with their plans. That's why I keep on stressing the importance of tuning in to guidance and as far as possible living in a state of grace or oneness with all life.

Individual Responsibility

An appropriate subject is that of individual responsibility. To what extent are we responsible for ourselves? For our immediate families? For the cosmic pool of souls as a whole?

The central part played by free will in the spiritual scene is the most important factor in providing answers to these questions. All souls have complete free will with absolutely no restrictions. How free will is exercised may lead to the imposition of restrictions, but that's a separate matter. Aware souls *never* interfere with the exercise of free will.

It follows that as a spiritual being with total free will, each soul must be fully responsible for itself. There can be no other answer. If any soul were to attempt to assume responsibility for another soul it would be interfering with that soul's free will.

There are certain circumstances in which physical responsibility has to be assumed; for instance, in the case of parents and children. The form of the responsibility could include caring, sheltering, feeding, clothing, etc. All this is usually done by agreement, as we have seen in earlier sessions. But it's a temporary arrangement which should not be allowed to obscure the fact that each soul has its own special, unique place in the cosmic design, and that no other soul can fill that place or decide how it should be filled.

Our immediate families, of course, form part of the cosmic pool of souls. Once the question of physical responsibility is left out of the reckoning it is clear from what I have said above that each soul can only take responsibility for itself. It cannot deny any other soul the right to take responsibility for itself. It's not a matter of choice; the possibility doesn't exist within the expression of God/love.

My answers to the initial questions bring up other questions; for instance, am I preaching a doctrine of self-centered individualism? Where does loving, unselfish service to others fit in?

The fundamental prerequisite for any soul seeking self-realization, including, of course, taking full responsibility for itself means that, ideally, it should never blame any other soul for whatever circumstances in which it may find itself. I don't mean articulating blame; I mean that no feeling involving blame exists. Paying lip service to this requirement or accepting it intellectually only is of no value spiritually; it's the feeling that matters.

If each soul, then, takes full responsibility for itself there are many effects; for instance, no grievances, no bitterness, no blaming, no dependence. No soul can achieve self-realization for another soul. That's something that each soul must do for itself, although, of course, it may be helped if it is willing and able to receive help. Which brings us to a second question.

There is often a lot of confusion about the notion of service to others, which springs mainly from a conflict between ideas of selfishness and unselfishness. At this stage it is advisable for me to define what I think are commonly construed as selfishness and unselfishness.

If a person thinks only of himself, does not in any way share with others of what he has, has no sympathy for others, never offers help, he is regarded as selfish. On the other hand, a person is considered to be unselfish who always puts himself last, thinks of the needs of others before his own, shares with others of what he has, and is always prepared to help others no matter the inconvenience to himself.

The question of motivation has, of course, to be considered where the unselfish person (as defined) is concerned. Why does he act as he does? Out of duty or love? Out of desire for reward (eternal), or recognition, or with no such desire? Motivation is obviously a key factor in so far as the effects of his behavior on his consciousness are concerned.

Each soul, as love, is a part of the whole cosmic love. Each soul, although it has its own individuality, is a part of every other soul. By developing its own awareness it also develops the cosmic awareness. The more it develops its awareness, the more its capacity to manifest itself as the love that it is grows. Love of its nature cannot be confined or limited. In other words, it cannot do other than share itself. The practical effect of this is that the aware soul cannot but be of service to others in whatever way it can. The only question, then, is what constitutes service or help.

I mentioned in an earlier session that help was continually flowing from the Father as part of the grand design. How much help is received depends on the readiness and willingness to receive help by those in need of help. The sacrosanct nature of free will is the key. I previously used an example of a woman who seemed to be about to throw herself into a river. I put the question, do you stop her? And my answer was no, if you are aware. I continued on to say that if she cried out for help, then that was a different story. The point is that as an aware soul it is not open to you to interfere with her in the exercise of her free will. I deliberately used a stark example to emphasize the point.

The dilemma, then, for any human being seeking awareness, is how to give help without interfering with the free will or the overall life purpose of any soul. Life on Earth is full of examples of people imposing themselves on others, or advising them in no uncertain terms what they should or should not do; or of people engaged in charitable activities. It is difficult in these cases to be objective and to be free from the pressures of conformity.

Predictably, my best answer is that the more consciously a person works with guides, the more he can be of service to others. Primarily, commitment is needed; commitment to allow oneself to be used as a channel of help, an instrument of love. This involves letting go of egotism which includes letting go of desire for recognition or eternal reward. Selfishness/unselfishness don't really figure in real service. One acts out of love in the only way one can act.

Guides: Guardian Angels

It's a strange thing that in all the centuries since human beings have inhabited the Earth their understanding of life has largely stagnated. Their vision of life has rarely gone further than life on Earth being a vale of tears to be succeeded by an eternity spent in adoration of a remote, patriarchal God with angels everywhere flapping their wings; or suffering horribly in a hell crowded with indescribably evil devils. That so many people have lived and still live with such a vision of life and death is a great tragedy. Through the centuries many wise and developed souls have tried to open people's eyes to their own greatness as spirit beings, but they have only succeeded in having themselves put on pedestals as saints or gods. Their intention was that others should be given a chance to share their vision and find what they had found. The more developed a soul is the less it wants to be put on a pedestal, and the more it reaches out with its whole being to help other souls to see what they are.

Now much is being done to spread among people the idea of continuity of life; not in the sense of judgment day and eternal heaven or hell, but as a growth towards a realization of each soul's integral unity with God. People are also being reintroduced to the idea that they have guardian angels, something that many used to believe as children but which usually fades as the concept of angels assumes a fairy tale or unreal image. Yet angels there are, and each person, if he so chooses, has at least one assigned to him to guide him through his Earth life. These angels are evolved souls who are familiar with Earth's conditions and who have already learned the lessons it has to offer. The choice is made before the soul's entry or reentry to Earth. The soul has free will to decide whether it wants a guide or guides to help it. It is a matter of agreement between them. Even though they have other work to do, guides are always available to the persons they have agreed to help; they are never more than a thought away. A person's free will is always sacrosanct. While the guides are constantly helping in all sorts of inspirational ways, they will not interfere unless they are asked to do so.

It has been said that to know yourself is the beginning of wisdom. To know that you have guides to help you through life is a stepping stone to wisdom. To tune in to your guides and to ask for their help is the achievement of wisdom. It would be a great mistake to think that in asking for help and advice from your guides in coping with the daily challenges of life you would in some way diminish yourself, or your capacity to make decisions for yourself. You cannot but increase your wisdom and decision-making capacity by reaching out towards a higher consciousness than your own. In a very real sense the more you tune in to guidance the more self-reliant you become because you begin to realize that you have immediate access to all the answers you need. Thus the living of life becomes a simple and enjoyable process. You are making the best possible decisions in harmony with the universal scheme of things and you know that you are doing exactly what you set out to do with your life.

People who choose to relive an Earth experience for the sake of repeating a pleasurable sensation or series of sensations usually do not wish to have guides helping them. However, if at any stage during their Earth lives they change their minds, there are many evolved souls willing and only waiting to be asked to act as guides. For such is the universal love of which we are each a part that we are only being true to our own natures if we help each other. And in helping each other we also, of course, help ourselves. None of us exists independently of another, which is often hard to accept in the daily commerce of living, particularly when a situation of antipathy arises between people.

I have talked about tuning in to guidance. How best can this be done? The easiest way is to set aside a little time each day, a little time of stillness, for communication with your guides. This needn't be the same time each day, it needn't be any particular time of the day; but no matter how busy you are you should make a point of having a few quiet minutes of communication. If you have particular problems to solve or decisions to make, meditate on them and ask your guides for their advice. Just wait for it. It will come, maybe in the form of words or a feeling or a picture, but it will come. With practice you will be able to do this automatically as often as you need to during the day.

How can you be sure that it's your guide or guides talking to you and not some less evolved or mischievous spirit? It is true that many souls do not wish to give up the influence they had on Earth and seek to control people by suggesting certain courses of action to them. Or well-meaning relatives may wish to continue to shelter their children and loved ones from the challenges of life. But if you make a conscious decision to ask your guides for help they will see to it that no other spirit can communicate with you without invitation on your part. Remember that you make the decision. If you don't ask for their help the guides cannot impose themselves on you. This is the nature of love; it never seeks to possess or impose. There is no limit to the amount of help available to you; if there is a limit it will have been set by you.

Does all this mean that if you have a problem you can simply ask your guides to help you solve it or to offer you a solution? Yes, most certainly. Don't just take my word for it. Try it and see.

I, in common with many others, feel that humanity as an experience will continue to stagnate unless it can be given positive direction from spirit. As I have emphasized, this can only be done with the conscious cooperation of those experiencing humanity. But what a marvelous world it would be if all were linked together in a cooperative effort stretching through all the stages of spiritual evolution.

I would like to draw attention to the traditional role given to angels, that of being messengers of God. And so they are, but they are more than that. They are the custodians of God in the centers of those whom they guide.

Guides: Helpers on the Journey

If you accept that you have guides helping you and that you planned with them your purpose in living this Earth life, it stands to reason that it is desirable for you to keep in regular communication with them. I already outlined a way of doing that. At this stage I feel that it would be well if I elaborated somewhat on the subject of communication with the aim of helping to make the fulfillment of people's life purposes as simple as possible.

What was the idea in providing guides at all? The ninety-nine percent (the Father) prepared the grand design which envisaged that all souls would help each other. Picture the way back to full awareness as a ladder. The ninety-nine percent are at the top of the ladder, and, in fact, designed and made the ladder; help is flowing downwards from them all the time to the souls on the various rungs of the ladder. Equally, as souls move up the ladder, they help those on lower rungs as far as possible. As outlined in the sessions on the seven stages of evolution, when souls reach the fourth stage, well up the ladder, they have progressed beyond the lessons of Earth while having experienced life on Earth, and can therefore be of great help to souls still going through the Earth experience. The grand design was formulated because souls weren't able to get back up the ladder, in many cases even to get onto the bottom rung, by themselves. As a soul reaches the stage of awareness of all souls being a unity he will want to stretch a hand downwards (metaphorically speaking) to help others to join him on his rung.

A soul who has not yet reached the fourth stage has not yet mastered fully the lessons of Earth and therefore can help others in a limited way only. Hence the idea behind choosing souls at the fourth stage as guides. They can see the full picture.

If souls could climb the ladder on their own, there would be no need for guides. Experience has shown that they cannot. This is as true of the souls who have climbed all the way back to the seventh stage as it is of those who are at present at the fourth stage or at any of the other stages.

Life on Earth wouldn't be possible at all if souls didn't help each other. People have no problem in accepting this at the human level because it is so obvious since, for instance, all people start their human existences as babies. Yet the idea of help coming from souls not in physical bodies is often unacceptable and even seen to be diminishing in some way. This is strange, but perhaps not so strange because, by and large, people only accept what they see, and since, as a general rule, they don't see spirits, it's not so easy to accept that they exist.

Why didn't the grand design make things easier so that human beings could see and talk to their guides? Wouldn't it be logical to expect that they would climb the ladder much faster if such communication were possible?

The answer to the second question is yes, it would be logical to have such an expectation; but whether the desired result would be achieved is open to doubt. Awareness tends to come about only through personal experience. In any event, the first question is the key one and the answer to it incorporates, among other things, the reason why we are doing these sessions the way we are.

I explained how the fall from awareness happened. The use of free will, that most vital and important attribute of spirit, was the central factor. The fall was not a dramatic one but rather a gradual process, and realization of its happening only came according as what was previously possible came to be impossible. For instance, what I might call inter-spirit total communication; in other words, communication which is only achievable between souls at the same level of awareness, became impossible. In due course communication of any kind between souls at different levels of awareness was no longer desired (as you will have seen happening with human beings) and ultimately the fact that such communication was ever possible came to be forgotten. With the fall from awareness came a residual resentment and suspicion of those who had not fallen, which survived and still survives in the subconscious minds of many, and forms the basis for the non-acceptance or downgrading of spirit communication including guides. Souls who are controlled by their subconscious are not comfortable with others who are not so controlled.

This is not so readily apparent in the human context. It is one of the advantages of the Earth experience that the physical cage serves as a leveler in that it provides a mask for the thought processes. Accordingly, souls of different awareness levels can communicate to a certain extent without resentment on the part of, and to the benefit of, the less aware. I say to a certain extent because the barriers obscuring communication are slow to fall and movement beyond the superficial is a matter of delicate timing.

The ninety-nine percent, in their wisdom, felt that it would only add fuel to the dormant (because forgotten) flame of resentment and suspicion if open communication with spirit was included in the grand design. Also, it was essential that freedom of will should be preserved; without it full awareness would not be possible. The right of choice is a basic ingredient of free will and consequently had to be built into the design. Freedom to exercise right of choice would be diminished if the way up the ladder were too plainly signposted by those who were already at the top of it or who had already fully or partially climbed it. But, above all, awareness grows slowly and from within; help, to be effective, has to be unobtrusive and measured to the capacity of the receiver.

Given that guides were built into the design and that their way of helping had to be unobtrusive, the best method of providing such help was through the glandular system of the human body. If conditions were right the guides could transmit thoughts in line with what had been agreed with the receiver before he entered into a physical body. All the guides' efforts are directed towards helping the person whom they are guiding achieve what he set out to achieve. There is never any interference with his free will. By suggestion the guides will try to keep the person being guided on course with his life purpose but they cannot (or I should say may not, if they are true to themselves in the state of awareness which they have reached) do more than that. So that's partly why I place so much importance on the development of two-way communication.

If you meditate on a particular problem, having asked your guides to come through to you with advice, how can you distinguish between your own imagination and whatever thoughts your guides may be directing towards you? Imagination is the expression of the mind. The mind and the soul are synonymous. Your mind (you, the real you) is in tune with your guides. (Your subconscious mind isn't.) Therefore, once you have asked for help, again I must stress the importance of asking because it's the expression of your free will, whatever comes through to you in meditation will be from your guides; your imagination and your guides are completely in harmony. So there's no need to worry about whether the answers you get are coming from yourself or your guides.

You can see now in a broader perspective the reason why so much importance is placed on looking within yourself for whatever answers you need. If you can do that, you'll always be in direct communication with your guides.

Why are some people able to see spirits, others able to see and hear them, others able to hear them or feel their presence, and yet so many others can do none of those things? There's a variety of reasons. Many people are frightened of what they regard as abnormal. Many don't believe in existence beyond the physical. Many think of anything to do with spirits as delving into demonology. Many have chosen lives of complete orthodoxy for specific purposes. Many are simply not ready for such manifestations. Ultimately, the answer lies in a person's chosen purpose in life. It doesn't necessarily have anything to do with a person's state of awareness, although conscious communication with guides cannot but be a help in increasing awareness; communication with other souls in spirit may be a help or a hindrance.

What I might call mediumistic communication with spirit can be risky because it may give free rein to the subconscious both in the medium and in the spirits coming through if the medium doesn't ask his guides not to let any souls through except by arrangement. There is no risk once the guides are asked to control the communication. After that, the fluency and effectiveness of the communication depend on the communicator and the medium. Once again, communication is greatly helped if the subconscious doesn't intrude.

I have emphasized the importance for each person of regular communication with his guides. This, in my view, is the key to growth in awareness in the simplest possible way.

More about Communication with Guides

As I have indicated, the best way to increase awareness is through regular communication with guidance. Because I am such an earnest advocate of communication, I feel that I should do everything in my power to show how the best possible communication can be achieved.

The first requirement is relaxation. If you're in a state of anxiety, communication (of any kind) is difficult.

How to relax? Stand, or preferably sit still. Take a few deep breaths, inhaling and exhaling gently. Let your mind go blank. Or imagine yourself in your favorite place doing what you like best to do, which may be nothing; or count up to, say, a hundred; or think of a very restful experience that you had at some time; or listen to music, if that appeals to you; or look at television, if you find that restful; or read for a little while; or take a walk. It's a matter of deciding what you find most restful and using that.

The next step depends on what form you wish the communication to take. If, for example, you would like to have some casual conversation with your guides you can do that simply by expressing your communications in thoughts and waiting for the answers which you will receive in thought form. If, on the other hand, you have a specific problem on which you would like the advice of your guides, it is desirable that you should first define the problem clearly. It is good for your awareness to try to define your own problems (I prefer to call them challenges or, better still, learning experiences) yourself. However, if you are not clear as to what the problem is or if you find difficulty in defining it, I suggest that you ask your guides to do it for you and to give you their advice on it also.

If you have already adopted the suggestion about asking your guides not to let other spirit entities invade your thoughts except by arrangement, then there's no more to be done.

To summarize, the steps are:

a) ask your guides, if you have not already done so, not to let any other spirit entities invade your thoughts except by arrangement with you;
b) relax, using whatever procedure best suits you;
c) communicate by way of transmitting and receiving thoughts; and
d) if you have a specific problem (learning experience) on which you need advice, try to define the problem first; if you are not able to do that, ask your guides to do it for you and to give you their advice on it.

If you follow these steps, you will find that with practice you will have no communication difficulties within a short period of time. I stress the words "with practice" because, as with every activity, there is no substitute for experience.

In conclusion, I would like to remind you that imagination is the language of the soul in case you might be inclined to dismiss valuable insights coming to you from your guides as being "just your imagination!"

PART III

The Physical Body

Here are three statements; one that is a matter of trust, but I hope also of reason, and two that don't have to depend on either trust or reason. A physical body is the agency that a soul uses for a lifetime on Earth; all bodies have common characteristics and features; they are divided into two categories, male and female.

Human beings were a product of the second stage of evolution. The pattern of male and female bodies and of physical reproduction were set at the first stage. The second stage is a development of the first, and the integrated soul needs a more sophisticated type of body than those provided at the first stage.

The body is a functional unit that operates according to an automatic pattern built into the overall grand design. The process of conception and birth, growth and decline happens as a matter of course that has come to be known as the natural order of things. Even when a body dies it is transformed into something else, dust or ashes, and is absorbed into the cycle of growth and rebirth. Nothing ever dies, in fact, only changes its form.

As the body is all that can usually be seen, it is a logical enough proposition that the body is all there is. By now, however, I would hope that I have established, even from a purely rational point of view, that life is a continuity of which the death of the physical body is merely a stage or point of transition on the way.

The division of the human race into male and female was not done solely for reproductive purposes. More important, the grand designers felt that the adjustments which each of the sexes would have to make in living and sharing with and understanding each other, as well as caring for and coping with their families, would provide a wider variety of learning experiences than would be available for one sex on its own. The overall grand design was, of course, envisaged before the first stage was instituted and the male and female elements were built into it from the beginning.

The physical pleasure which human beings get from their bodies is also part of the design. People often allow themselves to get agitated over so-called unnatural practices between human beings; for instance, homosexuality. As with pain, pleasure is only experienced by the brain that is neither male nor female. From a purely natural, as distinct from awareness, point of view, the stimulus that the brain uses as an immediate source of pleasure is of no consequence.

Practices such as contraception and deliberate abortion are regarded by many as interfering with natural laws and, particularly in the case of abortion, as murder. Obviously, these practices prevent births. Equally obviously, they don't interfere with the continuity of life since that is not dependent on physical happenings. No soul is in a position, or has a right, to make judgments about the practices or the people who perform them. Spiritually, the only importance that the practices have is their effect on individual awareness.

It is an inescapable fact that the physical body is subject to death. What is not generally realized is that, as a rule, souls not only decide on whether they will incarnate or reincarnate in a physical body, and the design of that body, but also on the timing and manner of the body's death. In reality, therefore, the death of the body is self-determined.

When life is seen in the context of its spiritual continuity the significance of the body can be put into its proper perspective. It is clearly important as a vehicle by which the soul has chosen to further its spiritual development. On the other hand, the disintegration or death of the body is no tragedy although, of course, the physical separation at death is a source of distress. Realization of the purpose of physical life on Earth and the relationship of the body to the soul should do much to lessen the distress.

Appearance in the Higher States

In the higher states of awareness the appearance literally mirrors the soul. The physical body is shaped in a particular way. Some bodies are more attractive to look at than others. What is it that constitutes a beautiful appearance? Regular features, a good physique, clear skin; all these things undoubtedly contribute, but above everything else, when one goes beyond the superficial impression, countenance is probably the most substantial ingredient. There are many examples of people whose physical features are unattractive but who are yet acknowledged to be beautiful, as indeed there are many examples of people who seem to have all the physical ingredients of beauty but who by general agreement are not beautiful. Obviously there is something that comes from within the person which produces or reflects beauty and which seems to be contained in the word countenance.

Imagine yourself in regular communication with a woman who has a severely disfigured face but who is, nevertheless, a most cheerful, positive, and admirable person in every way. After a while you are no longer conscious of her appearance, and if somebody meeting her for the first time remarked on it to you, you would probably react with surprise since you have become accustomed to seeing her as a beautiful person. What do you see when you talk to her? You see an impression that she, by her inner beauty, has created, and which, in fact, is the reality that she is. The physical appearance is irrelevant.

A typical example is a young mother growing old; her children are rarely conscious of her physical appearance until perhaps illness or infirmity affects her.

As I have said, there is no physical body, or no corresponding etheric body, in the higher states of awareness. What is immediately apparent is the impression that I referred to above, the real self. It is not obscured by any physical cage which is what a body is. Each soul creates its own distinct impression and is much more clearly identifiable, although in nonmaterial form, than a soul housed in a physical body. I can't go any further by way of verbal description. You'll have to wait to re-experience the reality to relearn what you've forgotten.

Feeling and Emotion

There is a distinction between feeling and emotion. Feeling is the real mind (soul). Emotion is the subconscious.

Since feeling and emotion are words which are juxtaposed and often regarded as synonymous in daily usage I will define them in my terms in order to clarify why I make a distinction between them.

Suppose you are a parent with a son. You observe him as he lies sleeping. You let the love that's in you for him flow towards him. You are not making any demands on him or in any way disturbing his harmony; you are uniting your harmony with his. That's feeling in action.

But then suppose that you start to think about things that could happen to him. What if he gets very ill and dies? Or has a bad accident? Or grows up to be a drug addict? Or can't find secure employment? Soon you will have allowed your state of harmony to be replaced by nervous tension, anxiety, worry, and fear. They are all emotion in action.

The distinction that I make between feeling and emotion is a bit superfluous in the context of common usage of the words. But my purpose in making the distinction is to highlight the influence of the subconscious in what I might call ordinary day-to-day life.

The regaining of full awareness means the elimination of emotion (within my definition of the word) and, accordingly of course, the subconscious. But in the transitional stages how does emotion, while it is still there, relate to God, or feeling and all its expressions? In other words, is emotion an expression of feeling even though an admittedly defective one? Yes.

To take an example: anger is clearly a lack of harmony and therefore an emotion. If you become angry and abuse or assault somebody you are giving expression to emotion. But you *are* feeling. What's happening is that you are behaving in an unaware manner.

In human terms there are many horrible actions being performed daily by people against people. These actions, horrible though they are, are expressions of emotion which in turn are expressions of feeling. They are actions performed by souls who are equal parts of God with their victims. The problem is that they themselves are victims of their own unawareness. ("They know not what they do.")

In the end everything comes back to the tragedy of the fall from awareness; all disharmony is a consequence of that.

But it happened, so what must be done is to restore the former position rather than to waste time grieving over its loss.

Conscious and Subconscious

The distinction between the conscious and the subconscious mind is generally a source of much confusion. Where does consciousness end and subconsciousness begin? And, most important, where does the subconscious end? Am I talking to you now or are you just using your subconscious mind?

It will be easier if I start with the last question first. You are conscious. You are aware of where you are, what you're doing, what's going on around you. Your mind is working normally. The only abnormal thing is that thoughts are flowing through from what you believe to be an external source, you are converting them into words and writing them down.

Consideration of this question is central to the whole arena of spirit communication, spirit guidance, guardian angels, and inspiration from whatever source. Creativity of any kind is involved; is the inspiration coming from the subconscious to the conscious mind or is there any external guidance? I know I'm talking to you and you know I am. But who am I? Am I your subconscious, part of your subconscious, your higher self (or lower self), or a separate individual? I am both part of you and separate. We are all part of God and God is a unity. Therefore we are all part of each other. At the same time we each have our own individuality. It's like a jigsaw puzzle (although this is a limited analogy). No two parts are the same and each part is indispensable to the whole. You are an individual personality and I am a separate individual personality. When that is applied generally then, of course, it means that all the kinds of communication I referred to earlier may come from separate spirit sources.

What then is the subconscious? It's the inactive part of the mind, the storehouse of memories and information of all kinds. It's like a computer data bank. At the press of a button (a shock, an emotional experience) memories are let loose, old feelings triggered off; what has been repressed comes to the surface. The subconscious may be rather similar to a (minor) sleeping volcano, which erupts on occasion pouring its lava in all directions. The more in balance a person is the less part the subconscious plays in his life. It is a mistake to think that any inspiration can come from the subconscious. It is no more capable of providing inspiration than a computer is, and, unfortunately, it cannot be controlled in the same way as a computer. It is desirable for all that they should eliminate the subconscious altogether by increasing the power of the conscious mind. Consciousness ends when the conscious mind gives over control to the subconscious, for example, when it allows fears and anxieties to take over. And subconsciousness ends, of course, when the conscious mind takes over positive direction of a person's life. The only demons in existence are creatures of the subconscious. Eliminate the power of the subconscious, tune in to guidance, and you will begin to appreciate the simplicity of life.

Conscious and Subconscious: Hypnosis and Dreams

I repeat that the more in balance a person is the less part the subconscious plays in his life. In other words, as a necessary step forward in the path to full awareness the subconscious should be eliminated.

All forms of mind control are exercised through the subconscious. The most extreme form of mind control is hypnosis.

There is a lot of confusion about what constitutes the mind, as distinct from the soul, the brain, the memory, or the imagination.

In spiritual terms the mind and the soul are synonymous. The mind is the real person, the source of thought and feeling. The brain is the physical mechanism which the mind uses in its Earth life. Memory is the mind's way of remembering things. Imagination is the expression of the mind.

In the earthly sense, the mind is usually understood to refer to mental functioning, whereas feeling is associated with the soul or the body. In the spiritual sense, the fully aware soul is a perfect blend of thought and feeling; the two are merged into one, which can be known as mind or soul if a verbal description has to be used. In my reference to the mind I am talking from the spiritual point of view.

People try to control others in all sorts of ways; physical, mental and emotional. In one way or another all efforts at control are directed at the mind. For example, fear only becomes effective as a means of control when it registers on the mind. But the mind (the soul, the real being) does not know fear; it's an emotion, as distinct from a feeling, and the real being is feeling rather than emotion, so it rejects fear as something alien to itself. If the mind is fully aware there is no difficulty because no emotion can reach it. The extent to which it is not fully aware, in other words the extent to which it is subconscious, is the extent to which it is subject to control.

The subconscious is, in effect, a memory bank of accumulated experiences which have been abortive as lessons to be learned and are therefore still undischarged, in a manner of speaking. Recurrences of the experiences, or similar types of experiences, trigger emotional responses in the inactive (unaware) part of the mind and add to the bank balance.

The subconscious is the source of all problems. (If there were no subconscious there would have been no need for the human experiment.) It's not much good trying to solve a problem without getting to the source of it; it's like treating a symptom rather than the cause of a disease.

How can the subconscious be eliminated? Different ways have worked for different people, including hypnosis. Given the sort of memories that are crowded into the subconscious, hypnosis can obviously be a very dangerous practice if used frivolously. But if the purpose is a healing one designed to get at the root of a particular problem, hypnosis can be very helpful. What it does best is to short-circuit the identification of areas of the subconscious, which are sources of difficulty; it may also, by suggestion, negate their influence. As with other forms of healing I would again emphasize that ideally hypnosis should not be used without checking with guidance and without the help of guidance.

I would not favor the use of hypnosis for regression purposes merely in the interests of trying to prove whether reincarnation is a fact or not. There may be damaging effects insofar as the persons placed under hypnosis are concerned. However, if regression is used as a basis for getting to the source of a present problem it can be very helpful, if done under guidance.

The subconscious tends to run riot in dreams. People are often puzzled as to why they have dreams that seem to them to be just a jumble of nonsense. The only significance such dreams have is that they point to a lack of balance in the dreamers. They are out of harmony with themselves and with life, in that they are living too much in their emotions. So, if you have dreams like that, relax, tune in to guidance, and find out where the imbalance is occurring; in other words, let light shine into darkness, illuminate and eliminate it.

Some dreams have, of course, a definite pattern and are a source of guidance to people, particularly those who are not aware or cannot accept that they have guides to help them. Generally speaking, if a person is in harmony and in regular communication with his guides he will not have dreams, although he may have recollections of astral traveling which tend to be confused with dreams. There's a simple rule of thumb by which you can distinguish astral traveling from dreams. If you remember having talked to people whom you know to be physically dead, or having visited particular places, or if the sequence of happenings is apparently straightforward rather than symbolic, you are remembering your astral traveling which is a regular occurrence in most cases. Dreams are usually either jumbled or symbolic. As I have said, the jumbled dreams are products of the subconscious. The symbolic dreams are their guides' way, or one of their ways, of trying to reach those whom they are guiding; the symbols are an aid to the development of awareness. They may seem to be wasted on a lot of people (as with all forms of teaching). In all cases, however, at some time a spark will ignite and in due course the flame of awareness will grow.

I started off talking about mind control and I have digressed somewhat into dreams, although the subconscious is a connecting link between the two subjects. Mind control is actually a contradiction in terms. The mind (soul) is free and it is not its nature to be subject to any kind of control (by control I mean the confining influence of another or others). While forms of mind control, such as hypnosis, can, as I have said, produce positive results, they operate negatively—like poison on poison in an antidotal sense. In my view, the best way to eliminate the subconscious, that is, to restore the mind to its full awareness, is for people, working with their guides, to be brought face to face with their fears and emotions generally in as conscious a way as possible through learning experiences. If they accept that their difficulties are stemming from the subconscious and that they are no more than phantoms of their subconscious, then they can face experiences designed to eliminate the subconscious with a learning attitude, and thus a repetition of the experiences will probably not be necessary.

The commonly asked question "Why do all these things happen to me?" is invested with a healing rather than a complaining significance when viewed in that light.

Dreams and Memory

As I outlined earlier, all life on Earth—stationary and non-stationary—is animated by spirit (God). Within that context, parts of individual souls (non-humans) and individual souls (humans) animate non-stationary or mobile physical life. The motive force in non-stationary life is the mind (soul); once that leaves the body, it (the body) has no mobility although it may still have life, like a person in a coma. A baby's body in its mother's womb has life but it doesn't have mobility until the soul decides to go into the body.

The soul is, of course, non-material, and the body is material. How does the material confine the non-material? You will remember that I said that the brain was the physical mechanism used by the mind during its Earth experience. The mind stays with the brain in the head; it has to or the body would cease to function in a mobile way.

The grand design is most accommodating. It provides that the body needs sleep in order to sustain it and this allows the soul freedom from limitation, usually for a number of hours each night. It may not wish to use its freedom to engage in what is known as astral traveling, but, as a general rule, most souls leave their bodies every night or whenever the bodies take their regular sleep.

A material cage does not inhibit the soul; being non-material, it has no difficulty in leaving the body. However, it is always conscious that the body may be subject to sudden awakening so it links itself to the brain and is able to return from its travels in an instant if necessary. Most people will have experienced waking up with a start at least once in their lives; what has probably happened is that the soul has returned too quickly and reactivated the brain suddenly.

What does the soul do on its travels? It may go to some place that means a lot to it; or it may meet with friends or relatives who are now in spirit. It may meet other souls who are also astral traveling in order to clear up a misunderstanding or to solve a problem or just to have a chat. It may go to seek advice or guidance from its guides or other spirit sources; or it may just let itself drift, enjoying its freedom.

While the body, including the brain, sleeps, the soul is still awake in its conscious and subconscious states. When the body is awake it is generally occupied in doing something involving at least a certain amount of concentration. When the body is asleep, however, there is no rein on the subconscious mind. The letting loose of its stored-up fears and guilts and anxieties causes disturbed or nonsensical dreams or nightmares.

If the soul can, through astral traveling, communicate direct with spirit, including its guides, why is it necessary for guides to send messages through symbolic dreams? Even if a soul may have lost contact with its guides, why can't the guides just approach it and say something like, "Remember us?" and take it from there? I explained why it is thought best that guidance be unobtrusive, indeed why it is necessary that it be so. Unless a soul seeks them out the guides will not impose themselves on it. At the same time they have undertaken to help the soul achieve its life purpose in whatever way they can, so if it doesn't approach them directly, they will seek to help indirectly. The use of symbols in dreams is one way because they may excite curiosity and thus questions and answers opening up a path to increased awareness. Though, direct communication is much simpler and better.

Why can't people remember dreams or astral traveling more easily? My definition of memory was that it was the mind's way of remembering things. It follows from that that memory does not cease with the death of the body in the same way as the brain does. It would also be logical to assume that if life is a continuity stretching back through eons, each person would have memories of events beyond his present lifetime. Yet most people don't have such memories.

The explanation is that the grand designers thought it best that souls should be given repeated opportunities to make fresh starts along the road to awareness. This was the origin of memory, as you know it. In its aware state the mind has access to all knowledge and has no need of memory. Because unawareness happened, some device had to be found which would both protect the mind from knowledge about itself and others, which would hinder its progress, and also help to bring to its attention matters which were necessary for its development. In other words, memory is a screen for the mind and is no longer operative once the mind regains its full awareness.

Broadly speaking, memory works in such a way that the mind remembers whatever it needs to remember at any given time. It is flexible and self-adjusting and during Earth lives it works through the brain (as one would expect since it is intricately linked with the mind). Accordingly, brain damage will obscure the memory during an Earth life but, like the mind, it will be restored to its former state after the death of the body.

If memory acts as a screen for the mind why do people remember nightmares or nonsensical dreams? What happens is rather like the soul getting back into the body and reactivating the brain too suddenly. The subconscious in control runs riot and in the process reactivates the brain. The memory is temporarily at the mercy of the subconscious until the conscious part of the mind asserts itself and assumes control. Dreams fade quickly from the memory once the conscious mind takes over. Making special efforts to remember dreams doesn't help awareness and in practice probably hinders it. The conscious mind will remember without effort whatever it needs to remember.

I realize that the whole business about mind and memory may seem rather complicated at first sight so I'll try to encapsulate it in a final paragraph. The mind and the soul are one. In the case of the one percent who lost awareness, the mind is temporarily divided into conscious and subconscious. The grand design of the ninety-nine percent (the Father) is aimed at getting rid of the subconscious. As a means of helping to achieve that aim the faculty of memory was introduced to screen the conscious mind from the effects of its subconscious, as well as from the burden of other extraneous material, which might make the way back to full awareness too difficult for it.

Memory: Do We Need It?

I defined memory as the mind's way of remembering things. I also said that it acts as a screen between the conscious and the subconscious and that it will no longer be needed once the subconscious is eliminated altogether. It is obviously rather difficult for you to conceive of a situation in which memory doesn't operate but I'll try to explain what it's like.

With the elimination of the subconscious the soul is no longer prey to negativity, such as fear, resentment, anxiety, worry, guilt, hatred. Its consciousness, or awareness of itself, and of its place in God, is complete. This doesn't mean that a fundamental or magical change takes place; all it means is that the remaining veils of unawareness are lifted and the soul is once more conscious of being fully and completely itself and at one with all souls and all life. The soul doesn't miraculously know everything. It does, however, have access to all knowledge since all knowledge is contained within the collective consciousness of all souls, and the aware soul knows where to find the answer to what it wants to know at any given time.

In your terms I know who I am which includes knowing what I have been and what I will be. I am a spiritual being of feeling from which follows thought. My thoughts which emanate from me—which are myself as an expression of me—lead me towards certain directions of interest; anything I want to explore along those lines of interest I can do by tapping into the collective consciousness. Thus I evolve. When I move from one line of interest to another I retain my knowledge of the first line although I may exclude it from my consciousness, if I wish, while I'm concentrating on the second line. I don't have any memory obstacle to overcome.

A parallel with your situation would go rather like this. Suppose that yesterday you researched a certain project. Today every detail is still vivid in your mind even though you are working on something different. While you are working you exclude yesterday's project completely from your consciousness; but, if you wish to do so, you can comprehensively recall all the details of it. Memory has not yet created a barrier to recall. To me all is as yesterday; or, more accurately, today. That is, in fact, total consciousness. Memory, or forgetfulness if you like, is no longer necessary.

Sanity and the Subconscious

It is not an uncommon experience for people to become mentally unhinged and lose the power of coherent thought at some stage of their lives. What happens to them if they die in that state?

Life is, of course, continuity. The mind doesn't undergo a miraculous transformation on the death of the body. All that happens is that it sheds its physical cage and is no longer subject to physical limitations.

I would define mental stability or sanity as a condition in which the conscious prevails over the subconscious, and insanity as a condition in which the subconscious prevails over the conscious.

Many people operate in a fifty-fifty state between the conscious and subconscious. This is a precarious state where a small tilt towards the subconscious will give it a controlling influence. Periods of depression, for example, or worry, or emotional outbursts, or religious fanaticism, or regular immoderate consumption of alcohol or drugs, or sexual obsession, or any similar conditions, can easily upset the delicate balance between the conscious and the subconscious; or, if you like, between sanity and insanity.

Even though most people experience periods of insanity during their lives they are usually able to get back to at least a fifty-fifty state. But in some cases the subconscious apparently takes over permanent control, and they are no longer able to communicate rationally.

The explanation in all cases comes back to free will. Souls perform certain activities that bring consequences. When they reach the second stage they have been brought up to a level of awareness where the mind is more than fifty percent conscious; in other words, the conscious is in control. By the use of their free will they either increase that percentage or decrease it. The struggle between the conscious and the sub-conscious continues through the agency of the free will. Usually a soul is ready to enter the third stage when the balance is about eighty-to-twenty in favor of the conscious. At the fourth stage the proportion of subconscious influence remaining is usually in the range of five percent to ten percent and certainly not more than ten percent.

A soul which lapses into insanity and leaves its physical body in that state may remain in it for some time; the length of time depends on the way it responds to the help being provided for it. This help takes many forms that are all geared towards building on the awareness that it already has, and reducing the extent of its subconsciousness.

Some forms of apparent insanity on Earth are caused by brain damage. I say apparent insanity since the brain is the physical mechanism that the mind uses for its Earth existence and, therefore, is no longer operative when the body dies. What happens in such cases is rather like an extended sleep condition; once the mind is free of the body it resumes its former state.

There is no need to be depressed about the fact that a soul may remain in a state of insanity for some time after the death of its body. As you know, conditions of insanity are often successfully or partially successfully treated on Earth by healing methods, including shock treatment. (I mention shock treatment because some brain damage may result from it, but this does not necessarily affect the mind in an adverse way any more than, say, damage to an arm or a leg.)

The Grand Design: Volume 1

If spirit beings can help each other on Earth they can also do so when they are no longer on Earth.

Once the subconscious is eliminated a soul has regained its former state of full awareness. At all the stages of development up to and including the sixth a certain element of subconscious influence exists. In some of the states of the first stage, the element of awareness remaining in the mind is virtually nonexistent, a fraction of one percent. Gradually, through the states of the first stage, the awareness is increased to where the soul is conscious of itself as an entity and is therefore ready for the second stage at which point the conscious is in control, even if only marginally so, and free will is again operative.

Mind Control

As we saw in the development of the explanation of God, all creation, while having its own separate existence, still exists in the mind of its creator, or more accurately, in its creator. The body owes its existence to the soul, which is temporarily using it as a vehicle for an Earth life. The soul designs the body along the lines that it considers best suited to its life purpose. The body doesn't have any motive force until the soul enters it and, of course, it loses that force and dies, or I should say is transformed, once the soul leaves it. It follows that the body is immobile without the soul, which is synonymous with the mind. Accordingly, the influence of mind (soul) over matter (body) is total.

So when people talk about mind control what they are really discussing, albeit unconsciously for the most part, is the direction of mind control. It is there *de facto*; how it's being exercised is the only point in question.

As we have seen, the brain is the physical mechanism used by the mind (soul) in an Earth life. Therefore, the agent

122

of control in the physical sense is the brain. Thus a person in a coma, for example, where the brain has been rendered inoperative, is temporarily mindless in the physical sense, although, of course, his mind continues to function as soul.

The brain, being physical, is subject to physical conditioning. It is open to the influence of its environment and the ideas generally, with which it comes into contact, including ideas about illness. For example, a child is taught that if he gets wet and wears wet clothes for any length of time he will catch a cold; if his conditioning has been successfully achieved, in other words if he believes what he's told, he will inevitably catch a cold.

What of a child that's born in a sickly condition; surely its brain has had no influence on that? Its brain, no; but itself (mind), yes, It chose that condition and presented itself with the challenge or opportunity of learning from it.

The mind feeds messages to the brain and gets messages back from it. That's how development or its obverse occurs during an Earth lifetime. The only thing that matters in the long run is the impression created on the mind.

You feed the beliefs that you have about the aspect of yourself that reincarnated in your present physical body into your brain. Your brain, in turn, is receptive to conditioning in its Earth environment, and feeds further impressions into the mind that may change or reinforce its earlier beliefs. Thus does your body serve your mind through its physical agent, the brain; thus in reality does your body serve you; thus are the opportunities provided by Earth existence put into effect.

A common form of conditioning, for instance, is that if a soul leaves its body in a state of sin it will go to hell, or certainly to some place of punishment whether temporary or eternal. The brain accepts the conditioning and relays it to the mind which enshrines it as one of its beliefs.

Another common form of conditioning is that a person needs six to eight hours sleep a night and that if he doesn't get that much sleep he'll feel tired the next day. So he will if he accepts the conditioning.

Now suppose that you experience some physical symptoms that suggest to you that you are unwell or malfunctioning in some way; for example, your eyes feel strained. The expected reaction in your environment is to have your eyes tested and as a result you will probably find yourself wearing glasses. The sequence is logical; your eyes feel strained, therefore you have them tested, you are supplied with glasses, and you believe from then on that your eyes are defective.

But, you say, the test showed that they were defective; that's a physical fact. Yes, and the provision of glasses will ensure that they remain defective. I want to make clear that I'm not making any judgment about eye tests or any other kinds of tests, or remedial practices such as wearing glasses. If wearing glasses helps people to have better vision, then the practice has its own merit. In the physical sense it can obviously, and in the spiritual sense it can possibly, be helpful if a natural faculty is aided by artificial means.

The advances made in this century in medical technology, as indeed in technology generally, have, ironically, reduced people's dependence on themselves. Even the most minor illnesses are now treated with drugs of various kinds. The result is, of course, that the remedial properties built into the design of the body are being destroyed. In physical terms it's a classic example of creation turning on its creator. Again I have to say that I'm making no judgment on technology in itself; it has its own important part to play in the grand design.

To return to the example of the defective eyes; what alternative is there to the provision of glasses if the person's visual capacity is to be improved? The common belief is that there's no alternative. For a person who accepts that belief, there is, in fact, no alternative. But the reality is that most illnesses or physical defects can be cured by the mind working through the brain.

The first step is to accept that it can be done; full acceptance is not easy because of the prevailing beliefs in many communities. The next step is for the mind to transmit its belief to the body through the brain and to do it repeatedly. If there is one particular area of the body, say the eyes, which seems to be defective, I suggest that a phrase such as "my eyes are perfect" be repeated for approximately five minutes each day for about fifty days. This repetition, if done with full acceptance that the eyes are perfect though not at present manifesting their perfection, will produce apparently miraculous results. The same type of formula can, of course, be used for any other part of the body. No, I haven't forgotten. Before doing any exercise of this kind it would be advisable to confirm with your guides that it will not adversely affect your life purpose in any way.

The body starts out with all the ingredients needed for the mind's purpose. Its life span is pre-ordained by the mind. Subject to the overriding priority of its life purpose, it is in the mind's best interests that the body should operate to its full potential. Therefore the mind's beliefs about the body, and its own relationship with and influence over the body, are important towards the fulfillment of its life purpose.

By what I'm saying in this session, I'm seeking to help souls to accept and fulfill the full potential of their Earth experiences. If they have difficulty about such acceptance it is better for them to stay with the traditional practices for as long as they find them supportive. Ultimately, in any case, they will come to an acceptance of the magnitude of their being; only the road will be longer and their feet will be more blistered, metaphorically speaking.

PART IV

Natural and Supernatural

I hope that the people who read these books will come to realize that there's no great mystery about life after all. Many people live in fear of what they regard as the supernatural or the paranormal. This expresses itself in different ways, such as fear of dying with all its attendant uncertainties, or fear of spirits, "evil" or otherwise. But, of course, since we are all spiritual beings, there is no death. It just so happens that some spiritual beings confine themselves in physical bodies for a time, and while they are so confined the density of the physical limits their vision. When they leave their physical bodies behind ("die") they will again resume communication with souls who are still in spirit; or they may have to wait until those souls, or some of them, come back from an earthly trip. The only differences between spiritual beings—apart from individual style, personality, etc.—are in circumstances such as having a physical body, temporarily or not, and awareness levels.

We are all supernatural or natural, paranormal or normal, whichever way you want to look at it. So there is no need to fear the "spirit world." No soul, whether in spirit or in a physical body, can influence you unless you allow it to do so. You are always in complete control of what you feel and think if you want to be. Once you accept that and apply it, you are re-entering your own kingdom as a free spirit.

It may seem somewhat disappointing to think of spiritual beings in spirit as "ordinary" creatures such as spiritual beings in physical form (human beings) appear to be. In that context, I need only mention the soul/oversoul relationship. You may, perhaps, find it helpful to think of the soul and oversoul as the natural and supernatural aspects of consciousness, respectively. So anybody who is afraid of the supernatural is really afraid of himself.

The Oversoul: What It Is

What is intelligence? The measure of capacity for receiving and retaining information? Mental alertness? I would define intelligence as that quality which enables a person to receive, understand, and communicate information. That I have included the communication of information may be somewhat surprising, but I think that it is a necessary ingredient. For example, it is not enough for a person undergoing a test or an examination to know the answers, he must be able to transfer his knowledge to the examiner in a readily understandable way.

Obviously, intelligence is a mental attribute. The mind and soul are one and the same; the brain is the physical mechanism used by the mind during an Earth life and the brain dies with the body. Intelligence is linked with the brain and, accordingly, is only operative during Earth existence.

The brain chosen by the mind (soul) for a particular Earth life is specially designed for its life purpose. The fact that one person is more or less intelligent than another is no indication of levels of awareness.

So we have a mind (soul) which chooses a particular type of physical body to fulfill a planned life purpose; the body incorporates a brain and the brain manifests itself through intelligence.

When the body dies, the mind (soul) is free of the body and free of the brain and the intelligence associated with the body. Does this mean that its mental condition may be completely changed? An example may help to clarify things.

Take a soul which in a particular life on Earth achieved fame as a philosopher and a writer. His writings were particularly notable for the clarity of his thought. All who knew him or of him acknowledged the superiority of his intelligence and his mental capacity generally.

In the course of time he leaves his physical body and returns to his former spirit state. He evaluates his present state of awareness and the contribution that his most recent experience on Earth has made to it. He finds that he has made some progress but that he has not succeeded in fulfilling his life purpose in that he has accepted other people's evaluation of him as a superior being. In order to counterbalance this he decides that he will reincarnate in a physical body with limited intelligence in an environment that encourages respect for those with high intelligence levels. So here we have the apparently incongruous situation of a man who was renowned for his intelligence in one lifetime being disregarded and downgraded because of his lack of intelligence in a later lifetime.

Once again he lives his life span and passes on. It takes him some time to adjust to his changed condition. He responds well to the help available to him from his guides and other souls. Soon he throws off the shackles of his most recent Earth condition and he is able to resume his former (mental) state with the added dimension accruing to it from his experience on Earth.

A useful analogy in the physical sense is that of a person who becomes blind during an Earth life. He is now operating with less than the capacity formerly available to him. Each and every soul that chooses to incarnate or reincarnate in a physical body is operating under restrictive conditions from which it will be freed on leaving the physical body. It will only retain the self-imposed mental restrictions.

The soul that presents itself to the world in a physical body only manifests itself to the extent that it has chosen to be restricted while it is on Earth. In its Earth manifestation it is really only revealing one aspect of itself with the other aspects in the background, although supportively so, while that one is being developed. When it returns to its spirit state it gradually reassumes all its aspects.

This is a rather difficult concept and I don't want to create any misunderstanding about it. There is no question of the soul being fragmented and a part of it being housed in a physical human body. It is just that, for instance, one particular quality is being developed and exclusively concentrated upon during a lifetime. If you think of an Earth lifetime as a training course you will be able to grasp the idea more easily. Say you attend a course dealing with a particular subject such as interviewing skills. During the course you are concentrating exclusively on the development of those skills. At the same time all your other skills and all that constitutes your being are still there and are, in fact, supporting you during the course; only while you are concentrating on the course you are not conscious of your greater, more comprehensive, self.

The soul on Earth is rather like a many-sided structure that is only showing one side of itself at a time. It remains the same soul when it resumes its non-physical condition, but now it rediscovers its other sides. Accordingly, life in spirit is much more broadly based than on Earth. While there are, of course, still different levels of awareness in the spirit world, each soul is revealing itself in full, and because of that is a more rounded and considerably larger being than it shows itself to be on Earth.

There are many records of spirit communications which depict souls in spirit as being essentially no different in their thinking and behavior than they were on Earth. This is true to the extent and for as long as they remain earthbound.

Each soul in spirit, no longer constrained by a physical body with its brain and intelligence, and having thrown off the scales of unawareness and accepted itself fully, is a much more magnificent and glorious being than it can possibly appear to be while in the Earth condition.

The Needs of Each Soul Are Unique

Reincarnation, that is, repeated expression of a soul in physical bodies, is a fact of Earth existence, which operates on the basis of a linear time sequence. The aim is to provide souls with as many opportunities as they need to enable them to reach a certain stage of awareness, or spiritual development. Life on Earth can be very helpful towards that end, but souls are free to choose other ways instead of physical existence on Earth in which to learn the lessons they need to learn.

The needs of each soul are, of course, unique. Initially all the souls (the one percent) who lost awareness went against their own natures and essentially no longer accepted themselves for what they were and are. So it can safely be said that, while the needs of each soul are unique, all unaware souls suffer from a lack of self-acceptance. This has led to all sorts of negativities. Some examples are fears, anxieties, tensions, intemperance, intolerance, superiority and inferiority complexes, mental disturbance, bitterness, hatred, prejudice, greed, cruelty, disrespect for others, ill-humor, frustration, envy, diffidence, arrogance, narrow-mindedness, bigotry, fanaticism, power-hunger, lust, pride, resentment, possessiveness, aspects of which affect each unaware soul to varying degrees.

As a general rule, a soul, in reincarnating into a particular body and environment, is concerned with eliminating an aspect, or at most two or three aspects, of its negativity or its subconscious. The number of times it will choose to reincarnate depends on its progress in fulfilling its purpose during a lifetime as well as the extent of its subconscious or unawareness.

When a soul reaches the stage where it is ready to incarnate, it is at least fifty percent conscious and certainly not more than fifty percent still subconscious. Its first incarnation will be aimed at reducing the subconscious by probably less and certainly not more than one percent. Thus it progresses and sometimes, unfortunately, regresses until eventually it is about ninety percent conscious, by which time it will have outgrown the lessons of Earth and will not need to incarnate any more.

Because each soul has free will, there was a risk that gains made in one lifetime would be counterbalanced in another unless life on Earth was designed so as to ensure that the gains could not be minimized in any way. Accordingly, it was arranged under the grand design that the conscious mind would stay put, or dormant, and would only send out an aspect or aspects of itself during a particular lifetime. In this way there is a bank of positivity (conscious mind) which remains unimpaired no matter what may happen during a lifetime on Earth.

An example may be helpful. An oversoul has reached a state of, say, sixty percent awareness (consciousness) with, accordingly, forty percent unawareness (subconsciousness) to be eliminated. One of the aspects of unawareness that remains is bigotry. With the help of guides it chooses parents and an environment and designs a body and draws up a life plan to enable it to get rid of bigotry. The physical body of the baby that will accommodate the soul is constructed with its brain as the agent of the soul part of the mind (oversoul). Memory acts as a screen for the mind and only allows it to remember what it needs to remember in order to help it fulfill its life purpose. The soul has all the style and characteristics of the oversoul but its mental range is limited by its brain and memory. Both the memory and the brain operate in such a way that, in a manner of speaking, a spotlight is focused upon the aspects of the soul (feeling and thinking) which are oriented towards bigotry. While this is happening the other aspects (the oversoul) are dormant.

It's as if you are concentrating exclusively upon a particular task. While you are thus engaged you are only using a particular aspect of your mental faculties; in other words, you have far greater mental capacity than is needed for that task. If time stood still and you were "frozen" in the performance of the task, it would seem to an observer that you have no greater capacity than you were revealing in the performance of the task. That's what life on Earth is like in spiritual terms.

The oversoul and the soul can be equated with you as you are, and you frozen in the performance of a particular task. In reality there is no distinction between the two but I have used the terms in order to show that each soul/oversoul is a far greater being than is apparent from its physical manifestations on Earth.

Soul (mind) is not a material substance and therefore the oversoul and soul are not like two separate bodies with one big one lying asleep while the other small one is out working. They are one whole but the major part of the whole is, as it were, playing a waiting game while the rest of it is developing itself. The development of the part will strengthen the whole; in other words, the mind will be freed of one more negative aspect (e.g., bigotry).

It is difficult for me to give an outline in human terms of the magnitude of the oversoul, a magnitude which continues to expand as the oversoul sheds its unawareness. However, you will get some idea of it if you imagine yourself with the mental capacity to understand without effort all the philosophical concepts that have ever been felt or translated into thought. Or imagine calling to mind, without having to cope with memory, all the poetry that has ever been created, or grasping immediately the most complex mathematical equations, or feeling the loving and creative impulses of all souls spreading into yourself. In other words, you see yourself as having an unlimited range of feeling and thought in whatever field you choose to interest yourself at any time.

The period of freezing, i.e., the period for which the soul is "away" from the oversoul, depends on how long it takes the soul to fulfill its purpose. It may be only one lifetime on Earth, it may be several, it may be a combination of life on Earth and life in spirit, or it may be entirely worked out in spirit. It all depends on free will and how the individual soul responds to the help it is constantly being given. Then, when that purpose is fulfilled, another aspect may need to be put right. If that is so, another soul will, as it were, go out from the oversoul until it, in turn, fulfills its purpose; and so on until the oversoul reaches a state where no more than about ten percent of its subconscious remains to be eliminated. At that stage there is no longer perceived to be any risk of regression and the oversoul brings its full capacity to bear on achieving the manifestation of itself in its former state of total awareness.

Total Awareness as a Goal

Why wait until the oversoul is about ninety percent conscious before bringing it fully into play in the elimination of the subconscious? Well, I suppose the obvious answer is that the grand designers felt that there would be a risk of loss of some of what had been regained; that the ninety percent threshold represented the point of no return. At that stage there is no predominant aspect of unawareness left. For example, an oversoul might have some traces of intolerance and pride and power-hunger and perhaps other negativities, but none of them would be present to any significant degree and they couldn't coexist for long with the overwhelmingly stronger positivities. When I use a proportion of ninety percent, I don't use it literally in the sense of clinical measurement. I merely want to show that there's a point at which all aspects of unawareness are reduced to such an extent that none of them is likely to gain any further strength at the expense of awareness already achieved.

I think that for the present we can leave aside the concept of soul and oversoul and I will use the term soul in talking about an individual being.

On the basis that many souls are still at a very low level of awareness and have a long way to go to reach even the second (human) stage, thousands of years, millions perhaps, are likely to pass before the grand design is fully implemented, if a time measurement is applied. That this should be so is, of course, a matter of much regret and concern to all those souls who are aware enough to know about the grand design and its progress. However, they are encouraged by the fact that progress is being made, albeit slowly, and that there can be no doubt about the eventual outcome.

If the whole operation is going to take so long, does writing down all this material serve any real purpose? From an egotistical standpoint it certainly doesn't, but that would only apply to you personally. Who knows how many people may come to be helped by it? There will certainly be enough time for that to happen. Only about ten percent of the people now on Earth have asked guides to help them with life purposes designed in conjunction with the guides; but if each of those were to succeed in fulfilling his purpose, the global progress, even in the brief duration of a lifetime, would be substantial. If some of the other ninety percent were to ask for guides to help them, the whole process of regaining awareness would be considerably accelerated. All they would have to do is express the wish because there are billions of evolved souls only too willing to help if asked to do so.

In case of misunderstanding I must explain that evolved souls are helping all souls who have not yet reached their levels of awareness, but, generally speaking, this is not being done as a conscious two-way effort. Many souls have very definite ideas about what they want to do with their Earth lives and they reincarnate with those ideas in mind. However, if they had asked evolved souls to help them design their lives on Earth they would be likely to find that their ideas would have to be moderated or developed or perhaps discarded altogether if they wished to raise their awareness levels. On the other hand, many souls reincarnate with nothing definite in mind; they just want to be with a particular group, or they have gotten tired of life in spirit, or whatever. To a large extent they may be wasting opportunities for growth. What I am advocating is putting such opportunities to the best possible use with harmony of purpose, the more advanced helping the less advanced in a progressive way.

Bringing Guides into the Picture

The soul on Earth is using the Earth experience to concentrate on an aspect of itself while all its other aspects are, in a sense, waiting around. You have seen in other communications, references to the oversoul sleeping while the soul is about its business. This is in essence the same idea, with the proviso that there is no separation between the oversoul and the soul; they are one entity.

Now it seems that some clarification is needed as to how guides fit into the new picture I have painted. For instance, if you have a problem on which you meditate, could the suggested solution not equally as well come from the dormant aspects of yourself, the oversoul, as it were, rather than from your guides?

Each soul has an inner knowing that there is more to it than it reveals at any given time to any person or group of people. Is that not so as far as you are concerned? That's what I was referring to when I said that the dormant aspects of the soul were always supportively in the background during an Earth lifetime. But these aspects—the oversoul, if you like—are really and deliberately dormant while the particular life purpose on Earth is being fulfilled or attempting to be fulfilled. If this were not so the whole purpose of the reincarnation might be nullified. Consider a physical analogy of one eye being covered up in order to allow the sight in the other to strengthen itself. Although for the analogy to be a reasonably parallel one, you would need to imagine a body with a minimum of fifty eyes with all of them covered up except one.

The image of the oversoul asleep is a very helpful one. While one aspect is being strengthened, the others are not in a position to influence, and perhaps retard by virtue of their overpowering presence, its development. One little eye might easily be neglected and allowed to weaken if, say, forty-nine others were beaming away all the time!

Thus what I have said in no way cuts across anything I have said previously about the part guides play in the whole design.

I am aware that in some other spirit communications there is either no mention of guides or they are not classified as advanced souls in the way I have done. All souls in spirit either already know about the existence of guides or are so informed when they are ready to receive the information. They usually forget this when they are housed in physical bodies, but they are reminded of it when the timing is right; either while they are still on Earth or afterwards. Whether they avail themselves of the help which guides have to offer is then entirely a matter for them.

There are many reasons why there is no mention of, or emphasis on, guides in some spirit communications. Some people like the idea of having guides, others don't. There are many roads to self-realization or helping others towards self-realization. None is necessarily the best one. The grand design accommodates all. I, and the others who are working with me on this venture, happen to think that the more souls who are aware of the existence and avail themselves of the help of guides, the easier the journey back to full awareness will be. They'll get there in the end anyway. We are hoping that we can help to make the journey less painful.

Mistakes Are Not Tragedies

The concept of the soul as a many-sided structure should be a source of encouragement (although I'm not too happy with the use of the word structure which implies rigidity; however, it serves for the purpose of illustration). Lack of progress in any one lifetime, although undesirable, is no tragedy since only one aspect of the soul is affected; all the other aspects are still in the bank, so to speak. Some people who believe in reincarnation worry that by using their free will in negative ways in a particular lifetime they will have nullified all the growth they may have achieved prior to that lifetime. There's no need for that worry, as what's in the bank cannot be touched during the lifetime in question.

For example, suppose we look again at the philosopher posited previously. Assume that his latest lifetime was a litany of negativity. Thus he failed entirely to fulfill his life purpose and the aspect of soul that he hoped to strengthen was, in fact, weakened. He will have to try again either through reincarnation or some other way, but the progress he made in other areas is not diminished. His ultimate return to full awareness is delayed because his latest lifetime represents regression to that extent.

Reincarnation would be very problematical indeed if the progress made by a soul prior to a physical lifetime was put at risk.

So now you're curious about how you as a soul relate to you as oversoul. As always, we're faced with the consequences of trying to put a concept into words. Soul and oversoul don't exist as separate entities. So you, as you are now, are also you as oversoul. It's just that there's a lot more to you than you think. It's as if you were a big mansion of which only one room is being used at present. That room was in a bit of a muddle and now you're getting it sorted out.

But, you say, maybe there are other rooms also in a muddle and you'll have to go through several incarnations or other undesirable processes in order to sort them out. This is an important point that may be best clarified by an example.

A soul reaches the second stage and is now once again exercising its free will. It has already got about halfway back to full awareness and has that much in the bank. It decides to incarnate as a human being. It has a lot to learn, or, more correctly, to unlearn. It has no chance of fulfilling all its needs in one Earth lifetime. With the help of guides it draws up a plan for an Earth life designed to meet some of its needs. The life goes exactly as planned. It is reviewed with guides and the increase in the bank (the area of conscious mind) is observed. A plan for a further Earth life designed to eliminate more of its subconscious area of influence is drawn up. Once again the life is exactly as planned. Progress continues more or less according to plan through a number of Earth lives with the proportion in the bank increasing all the time.

Then things don't go as planned in one life. The particular areas of subconscious influence involved are not only not cleared but are reinforced. Subsequently it takes the soul two Earth lives to clear them. This pattern is repeated in later lives. Eventually the soul progresses beyond the second stage, although in doing so it has had to undertake many more Earth experiences than would have been necessary had it managed to follow its plan fully in each Earth life.

So the position as to how many rooms in a mansion are still in a muddle varies with each mansion (soul). How to find out what your situation is? Just ask your guides and wait for the answer. However, I suggest that you decide whether you really want to know the answer.

Mastery of Further Aspects

We have already discussed the soul in relation to the oversoul, with the soul representing an aspect of the oversoul. If we accept that the soul incarnates or reincarnates manifesting a particular aspect of the oversoul, is it possible that a further aspect, or aspects, of the oversoul can be added during an Earth lifetime? In other words, could the oversoul keep on manifesting itself more and more within the one body to the extent that at some stage it would be totally present within that body? Yes, but in practice, only to a certain extent within the potential of one lifetime and the restrictions of one physical body. What often appear to be sudden expansions of consciousness take place, sometimes rather dramatically, at different times in the lives of some people. New understanding dawns. Former ways of thinking and acting are discarded. People often wonder how they could have been like they were before, how could they have been so rigid, so intolerant, so narrow. The simple answer is that they are really different people, or, perhaps, "expanded people" would be a better way of putting it.

As I have explained, when the oversoul sends out an aspect or aspects of itself (a soul) for growth purposes, what remains behind is rather like a bank of consciousness. (I hope that's a relatively simple way of understanding the concept of the oversoul.) Accordingly as the soul progresses positively on its earthly mission, the way becomes clear for the oversoul to allow itself to manifest more and more fully on Earth. However, in order to ensure that there is no diminution of the bank of consciousness already regained by the oversoul, a further aspect, or aspects, of the oversoul can only manifest when the soul has already mastered its original mission. It would be the ideal objective of each oversoul that it would regain as much as possible of its lost consciousness during the span of an earthly lifetime.

The Oversoul, the Higher Self, and Guides

People sometimes seem to find difficulty in reconciling the concept of guides with that of the higher self or the oversoul. And, indeed, are the higher self and the oversoul one and the same thing?

The oversoul is the total you. It sends out an aspect of itself, the soul, to increase its bank of awareness. As (if) the

soul grows in consciousness during its Earth life it inte-
grates itself more and more with the oversoul, which, in my
terminology, is the higher self. (Incidentally, I don't like the
description "higher self" as it implies the existence of a lower
self. The self is, of its nature, divine and, therefore, does not
lend itself to categorization into higher or lower definitions;
accordingly, I prefer to use the word "oversoul.") There is
never total integration during an Earth lifetime, although
some souls, rare exceptions, have come a long way towards
it. The physical body wouldn't be able to cope with the full
energy of the oversoul.

The function of guides (guardian angels) is to help the
soul integrate as far as possible with the oversoul. Guides
don't give instructions or directions; their role is to guide,
not command. The giving of instructions or directions in the
sense of mandatory commands would be an interference
with free will. The guides give guidance to those who are
open to receive it in order to help them along the path of
increasing awareness. The guidance tends to become subtler
and less straightforward as awareness increases.

There has never been, nor is there now, any person on
Earth, no matter how evolved, who did not, or does not, need
help. Each person begins life as a child, with total dependence for survival on another or others; and all through its life
on Earth that person has to be helped in different ways by
many people. The giving and receiving of help are so much a
feature of the daily routine of life that they don't need any
comment, other than that payment for services rendered
often obscures the fact that both the services and the payment are part of the processes of giving and receiving help.

It stands to reason that if people need so much help with
the physical aspects of life, they also need help with the non-
physical, or spiritual aspects. Guides are there to help with
all aspects of life. They make the process easier. Souls have

free will. They don't have to have guides to help them, but their journeys back to full awareness will be longer and more painful if they don't allow themselves to be helped along the way. The grand design was framed as a vast cooperative effort with souls at higher levels of awareness helping those at lower levels, subject, of course, to their being willing to receive help.

The oversoul in its ultimate (former) state of full awareness has access to the totality of (divine) consciousness. It *is* that consciousness, but, of course, is not all of it. What I want to bring to attention in this session is that, in the case of people who are still working through Earth lifetimes, the oversouls have not yet regained total awareness. They, therefore, still need help in the development of their relationship with themselves, and with God/love/feeling and all its expressions.

My approach is basically uncomplicated. If there's a choice between a simple and a difficult way of achieving the same result, choose the simple way. If you have luggage to carry, it's much easier to let it be carried for you by whatever mechanical means are available to you than to carry it on your back. Your guides will help to relieve you of the burden of unawareness if you allow them to do so. Then you will find yourself, you as oversoul, in the fullness of awareness sooner. It's always nice to find something you lost, isn't it? Not to mention something as valuable as yourself!

If you keep in mind the simplicity of no separation—unity, God is all, all is God, we are all in God—you will find that the complexities of compartmentalization, guides, higher self, oversoul, etc. fade away. Then it will be easier to allow all the evolved energy of the universe to support you in every way.

Time and Space

If people can get to the stage of being divine consciousness and acting out of that feeling, isn't that the last word? Would saying any more than this only lead to repetition and confusion?

How about looking a little further at the notion of time and space? Time and space, as you know them, are a feature of Earth only. In the world of spirit there's no time or space, just continually evolving consciousness. You know the feeling of no time when you're totally absorbed in, say, a pleasurable experience and you're free of any pressure of having to be somewhere or to meet somebody at a particular time. That's the nearest I can get to an analogy which may make the idea of existing within a timeless and spaceless experience understandable to you.

Over and over in our sessions the aim of unity, no separation, is fostered. Why, then, did the grand design make things so apparently complicated by having different systems in operation in the worlds of spirit and Earth when the purpose of life on Earth seems to be to bring the two together so that Earth is ideally an aid to the spiritual? Death is the answer.

The death of physical life allows transition and growth with the possibility of fresh starts. The linear time and space framework enables an aging process, which is not a feature of nonphysical life. Thus the body deteriorates and eventually gives up. The soul is then in a position to have a look at how it evolved during its Earth life; and, if it seems desirable to do so, it can, in due course, decide to have another try without burdening itself with conscious memories of past attempts.

Earth is an illusion in the sense that, in eternal terms, it has no reality. It provides a platform for physical happenings such as, birth, growth, varying experiences in between birth and death, but the happenings pass and are only important ultimately in the effects they create. The soul exists, and continues to exist, whether within a physical cage or out of it, and expresses itself through its feelings and thoughts, which is how it creates its reality, its own universe. Ultimately, then, feelings and thoughts are the only reality. We are our feelings and thoughts. Thus there's no physical limitation to us, we don't age, we don't die, we just evolve in consciousness. Time and space are a measurement of limitation that only applies to physical bodies and the physical environment.

A big challenge, which is coming more into focus at present, is how to merge the timeless and spaceless dimension of spirit with the time and space framework of Earth. One of the factors that made progress in the Earth experiment so painfully slow has been that the expression of spirituality has, particularly through religious culture, tended to imply rejection of the physical or material, including, often, the physical body and its functioning. Sacrifice, penance, self-denial, led to holiness, which was the ideal objective of spiritual searching. Because of the lack of understanding of the continuity of life and, within that, the purpose of life on Earth, it didn't register that rejection of the physical made nonsense of being born into Earth. Life on Earth has no point if the physical world, including physical bodies, is not seen as an aid to the spiritual and not as something separate from it. A soul that rejects its physical body is negating its opportunity for growth through Earth experience and might as well not have bothered coming into Earth at all.

Yet, rejection of the physical in pursuit of the spiritual has had its own logic. By withdrawing from the physical and transcending it one could free oneself from its limitations, which tend to be reinforced by time and space. One could enter into a meditative state where time would cease to have any meaning and where all the day-to-day problems of life fade into insignificance and where even eating for survival becomes largely irrelevant. The difficulty, as I see it, with that approach is that it is essentially an avoidance of the Earth experience. That's why so many souls who have followed that path in previous lives are now extending their search into the hurly-burly of daily participative living on Earth, and are not finding that easy. They tend to find the pull of "getting away from it all" particularly strong.

So trying to reach more into the timeless and spaceless dimension of spirit by running away from the time and space framework of Earth doesn't work in the long run. "I have no time for myself. I have no space. I need to get away. I need to be somewhere where there are no people making demands on me . . . no telephones . . . no clocks . . . no contact with all the problems of life . . ." and so on; these are familiar expressions of response to pressures of time and space. People are stressed because of their work, or because they have no work. They haven't enough time, or they have time on their hands. Or they are in confining, difficult relationships or situations and sometimes the most desirable, if extreme, solution seems to be to end it all, to escape into a hoped for oblivion of nothingness. But, in reality, there's no escape. Any new relationship or situation will bring the old with it because, ultimately, it's a matter of consciousness expressed through feelings and thoughts. Time and space are irrelevant where consciousness is concerned. It exists outside of them and is the continuing link between the world of spirit and the world of Earth, so that, in fact, they are all one. As one reaches that awareness there's no longer any relevance to the idea of getting away from it all, because the "it all" is internal.

In practical terms, then, how does it work? How does a human being meet the challenge of merging the timeless and spaceless dimension of spirit with the time and space framework of Earth? First, by accepting that he is a soul, a spiritual being, temporarily using a physical body, and that souls do not age nor are they confined by space. And, second, by realizing and accepting that the soul expresses itself through its feelings and thoughts and that, therefore, all the happenings of the Earth experience are only important in the effects they create on those feelings and thoughts.

All that does not mean that a person will not, or should not, participate fully in the human experience. In fact, through that acceptance he will find much greater freedom in participating in, and enjoying, the experience of Earth. His awareness will be expanded. He won't assume limitations of time, such as aging, or space, such as location. In short, he will be able to call himself a free spirit and know that he is truly so. He will understand and accept that governmental systems, religions, social conventions, are all just transitional ways of ordering and controlling behavioral patterns, and he can be totally free of them while ostensibly living in conformity with them, if he so wishes. He will not allow himself to be boxed in, to be categorized, to be labeled, to be limited by definition. He will play the game according to its rules, but he will know that it's only a game. In the true spirit of the game he will know that it's how he participates in it that's important.

Just as he will not allow himself to be categorized, etc., equally, he will not categorize others. By granting himself freedom, he also extends it to all others, without exception. No longer will he judge himself; no longer will he judge others. There's no yardstick for judgment when there are no definitions. The boundaries are gone, there's no time or space, the spirit is free to be, to express itself as it is. It reaches out to hug and embrace the whole universe with all the warmth, the joy, the simplicity, the comprehensive and glorious infinity of its unconditional love.

Time and Space in Relation to Guides

A question on which you'd like elucidation is, "How come time and space mean nothing to our spirit guides when they have probably evolved through human lifetimes?"

It's a fact that time and space, as you know them, are a feature of Earth only. They are expressions of structure and, therefore, limitation. The world of spirit exists outside of structure and, accordingly, is unlimited in its expression.

Guides retain memories of Earth and its structures and, of course, those memories help them in dealing with human beings. You might say that it's an ironic thing that souls come from the timelessness and spacelessness of spirit into physical bodies confined within the restrictiveness of time and space and that they have spirit guides who have themselves left that restrictiveness behind and yet see it as a positive thing that the human beings whom they are helping should be subject to the restrictiveness. You see, though, what the guides are doing is trying to help their temporarily human friends to reach more and more feeling of the freedom of spirit within the confined conditions of Earth, and they can do that more effectively because they are free spirits themselves. One of the reasons why souls can gain considerable benefit from adopting human form is that they have allowed themselves to become limited by structured thinking. By coming into that type of environment they are, ideally, brought up against the effects of such thinking. Whereas in spirit, because vibrations don't mix in the same way as they do on Earth (in spirit, like tends to associate exclusively with like), they might continue to exist within an unchanging framework of thought indefinitely.

It's not that time and space mean nothing to guides, it's that they are not limited by their rigid structures and they want to convey the feeling of their freedom of spirit to their human charges. At the same time, it's fair to say that, in being free themselves and in becoming accustomed to that way of being, it takes an effort for them to attune themselves to an environment that exists in such a structured way.

An illustration might be helpful. Suppose you hear about a community comprising a number of people who decided to "get away from it all," to establish a lifestyle for themselves where they are totally free to do what they want to do, even if that means doing nothing at all. They are in the fortunate position that they have in their younger years acquired enough money to be free of material worries. The only meaning that time has for them is that day passes into night and night into day. They have no clocks or calendars to mark the movement of time through days into weeks and months and years. They deliberately seek out and find a location where the climate allows them to live within houses or without them, as they wish. While they are still, as human beings, confined within physical formations, such as their own bodies, they are accustomed to feelings of spacelessness, the sort of feeling that one gets from gazing at the vastness of the sea or the seemingly endless range of the sky. They are no longer controlled by the limitations of space.

Suppose that you feel that you'd like to sample that way of life. You understand that the community has no rules and regulations and does not apply any process of selectivity; it's open to you, or anybody else, to swell its numbers. You are completely free to come or go as you wish.

You join the community and the lifestyle suits you very well. Soon (since you've lost track of time, you don't know how long), your previous way of life becomes gradually a hazy memory for you. You can still recall it, but you have moved into such a vastly different path that the details are shrouded in a mist of what is now an unreality for you.

Suppose that a colleague from your earlier life comes to visit you and starts discussing with you matters that previously would have been of gripping interest to you. Now, however, you find that you're seeing those matters in a totally different light. You approach the interaction with your former colleague both from his perspective in so far as you can now bring yourself to identify with it (and that identification is helped by your background knowledge), and also from the broader perspective of your present way. You still know about time and space as they are structured within his world, but they mean nothing to you in your life as it now is.

The above illustration is intended to convey that there may be circumstances even within the human condition where notions of time and space as commonly understood may have no meaning. I don't want to imply that an ideal way of living on Earth would be to establish or join a community such as the one I have described. It may be, for some; it all depends on what souls wish to learn from their Earth experiences. In fact, it is likely that for most souls, participation in the experiences of Earth, in all their restrictiveness, is the best way to achieve growth in consciousness.

Awareness

Earth is a training school that allows experiences designed to increase awareness. I agree entirely that to be aware is, among other things, to be without the scars of accumulated experience. The path to awareness, full awareness, involves getting rid of the scars; but in order to get rid of the scars one must learn the lessons which life throws up. Learn but not accumulate as a feeding ground for the subconscious; learn and leave behind.

Insofar as religious practices are concerned, souls are at many different levels of awareness. They can be helped in many different ways including the practice of religion.

In the final analysis nobody can increase your awareness but yourself and only by looking within can you do that. But you can be helped in many ways; and, as I have suggested, constant communication with your guides is, in my view, the best way. Is there a danger that you would use them as a crutch by, in a sense, passing on all your problems to them? No; they will help you to solve your problems in such a way that your awareness will be increased. You achieve harmony with all life. Once you're in harmony you're in *your* place, free of all others, not interfering with their freedom in any way. If you're out of harmony, you suffer from a lack of freedom and you are diminished to that extent. By putting yourself into harmony with all life you allow yourself to be fully open to the spirit which animates all life (God), of which you are a part and without which you could not *be*. The guides are channels of that spirit, as you are also, and all souls to the extent that they allow themselves to be. To be fully in harmony is to be completely open as a channel of spirit as well as a part of spirit, something like a link in a chain. On its own, a link is of little consequence; as part of a chain it has strength and purpose.

First Stage: The Purpose of Non-Human Life

Referring to our sessions on the seven stages of awareness as I categorized them, some elaboration on the first stage might be useful.

The first stage stretches from virtual non-awareness to a fifty-fifty state. This is the stage in which the soul is still fragmented, the non-human stage.

Because free will is not operative at the first stage, all activities follow the original pattern laid down in the grand design. Many souls at different levels of awareness have taken on specific responsibilities in connection with the implementation of the grand design.

You may wish to refer to the stages of awareness in order to refresh yourself on how fragmentation occurred and how the way back to awareness is being orchestrated by the grand design.

Within the various forms of non-human life there are gradations of awareness and souls progress through the different forms in a most comprehensively planned way until they reach a state where they are ready to integrate as individual souls and incarnate as human beings if they so wish. There is no element of chance in the non-human condition; things happen according to plan. Human beings interfere with the plan from time to time, especially by acts of cruelty, but adjustments are made to compensate for such interference.

A soul that has virtually lost all awareness is likely to incarnate in a multiplicity of physical bodies with short life expectancies. During its physical manifestations it will have made enough progress, mainly through the development of its instincts, e.g., for survival, for comfort, for food, to be ready to incarnate in another species.

All the different species of non-human life were specially designed as vehicles for increasing awareness and are classified in order of ascending level. The needs of each soul were thoroughly explored and a plan was drawn up for it. The progress of each soul is monitored on an individual basis. It is no exaggeration to say that nothing happens, even the most apparently infinitesimal thing, which is not comprehended by the grand design either in its original planning or by adjustment. Once a species has served its purpose it becomes extinct.

The most numerous forms of physical life are found in the insect world. The least aware souls progress through perhaps several species of insects. Fish, bird and animal life intermingle in the classifications. The highest levels of awareness are reached, as you would expect, at the stage of domestic animals, such as dogs and cats. At that stage a soul has developed from multiple fragmentation to, usually, five or less; in other words, a soul may manifest itself temporarily in the physical bodies of, say, five dogs or cats, sometimes maybe only two. If there is enough love shown to them in their homes, they are likely to grow sufficiently in awareness to become reintegrated as one soul.

Many people will find it hard to accept that as souls (spiritual beings) they may have progressed through physical life forms which they find, at worst, repulsive and, at best, lovable but mindless. I would suggest to such people that they ask themselves what purpose they see behind all the different species of life and how has it come about that there is such order and harmony in their world.

From an awareness point of view it is very important that the place of non-human life within all life should be recognized and accepted. It is also very important that each individual animal, bird, etc., should be treated with respect and love. It is just as important that humans should respect and love non-humans as they should respect and love each other.

Style

Given that each soul is unique and has its own special place in the cosmic scheme of things, what is it that gives it its uniqueness?

If one observes any gathering of people, it is possible, straight away, to see that no two of them look exactly the same unless there are identical twins in the gathering. Even with identical twins, acquaintance will reveal differences both in appearance and in qualities which distinguish one from the other.

On the human level there is, or should be, no difficulty about seeing the uniqueness of each person. However, acceptance of this uniqueness is often arrived at only after much misunderstanding and suffering both in communities and also in families. There are all sorts of physical differences as well as mental and temperamental ones that are usually obvious.

On the spiritual level the differences are not always so obvious. Essentially they come into the area of awareness and its different stages. I have said that each soul retains its individuality at the ultimate stage of full awareness while at the same time forming a unity with all other souls. What are the constituents of individuality in the ultimate sense?

I can encapsulate my answer in one word: style. By style I mean the way of feeling and thinking and of expressing those feelings and thoughts.

One of the big problems on the human scene is that so much time is devoted to knocking the style out of individuals—that is, their own style—and making them conform to somebody else's. As awareness grows, the development, or I should say the expression, of individual style is encouraged until ultimately there's no barrier to its expression.

Perhaps the simplest answer I can give to the question I posed at the beginning is that uniqueness is a matter of style which in the end comes down to being oneself without constraint of any kind.

Mission/Purpose vs. Free Will

A question recently put to you was "Is there a contradiction between arriving on Earth with a mission/purpose and the exercise of free will?"

It is understandable that there might seem to be a contradiction but, in fact, there isn't. It is because they have free
will that souls have opportunities and choices in designing
broadly the purposes of their lives on Earth. No soul is ever
forced to live a life on Earth; even a suggestion of compulsion
would be an interference with free will. If a soul decides that
it wants to experience a (further) life on Earth it is entirely
open to it to design its own purpose in as generalized or specific ways as it wishes. The soul has, of course, help available
to it in the form of guides if it would like to avail itself of their
help; that, too, is entirely a matter of choice. To the extent a
soul avails itself of the help of guides the greater will be the
potential for growth in awareness of a life on Earth.

The exercise of free will, then, is always sacrosanct. A sense
of mission or purpose, which some people have very strongly, is
a result of a choice freely made. How the purpose is fulfilled is
also dependent on the exercise of free will. In so far as a soul's
life on Earth is concerned, once it takes on a body and arrives
on Earth the only predestined element is that the body will die.
All its experiences between the birth and death of the body are
governed by free will on its own part and/or on the part of others, such as, parents, teachers, and religious authorities. The
design of its purpose will take account of environmental conditions, usually to the extent of the conditions being deliberately
chosen in order to assist the achievement of the life purpose.

Part V

Reincarnation

Reincarnation fits into the perspective of continuing life. It is a subject which has always been a source of fascination for some and is now of growing importance to many.

I don't want to get into an involved discussion about time. My aim is to simplify. It's a difficult concept for a human being to understand time in terms of a continuing present rather than in the familiar terms of past, present, and future. Both are valid concepts in their own way (in their own time, if you like!). If you think of time in a global sense put into the context of a world in the round, you will get some idea as to how the two concepts can merge. Then the past and the future come together into a series of recurring presents although often looked at from different points of view or reacted to in different ways. The division of time into seconds, minutes, hours, days, weeks, months, seasons, years and so on, with season running into season in regularly repeating patterns, illustrates the concept of time unfolding in a framework of change yet recurring sameness. I'm sorry if this sounds complicated but it is necessary for me to try to get across the idea of time as a vast continuing process which is not limited in the way that earthly divisions, and, indeed, the finality of limited earthly life-spans condition human beings to believe.

Reincarnation is a fact; that is, it is a fact that souls choose to repeat Earth experiences as part of the process of spiritual development and even sometimes just because they want to relive certain experiences in physical bodies. There is no more mystery about the fact of reincarnation than there is about rose bushes repeating the growth of roses. In what I have said about time, there is an argument for stating that since all life is lived in a continuing present, there can be no such thing as Earth lives following each other in a linear time sequence. It is not necessary, indeed it is undesirable, to concern ourselves with such an argument because the reality is that human beings have to live their lives within a linear time sequence. But at the same time it is highly desirable that in the larger context of spirit as opposed to physical existence they should be aware of an unlimited concept of time. A simple way of keeping this in mind is to remember that you are spirit temporarily limited by the constraints of existence within a physical body but that you have chosen the condition for a particular purpose and that the constraints are learning experiences.

So, reincarnation is a fact of physical existence. Some souls choose to reincarnate more frequently than others. The number of physical incarnations that a soul may have is no index to its progress in spiritual development. Reincarnation is only one way towards spiritual development; there are many others and some souls choose not to incarnate or reincarnate at all. This explains the often conflicting information coming from spirit sources about reincarnation. Some are simply not aware of it in the vibration in which they exist.

Because every soul has free will, reincarnation can have positive and negative effects. On the positive side an Earth life can be a particularly good developmental experience because there are so many challenges to be met, e.g. illness, poverty, wealth, conditioning. The soul that uses its environment positively will gain much. On the other hand, the soul that reacts negatively to its environment, say, embittered, bigoted, intolerant, or merely with passive acceptance of conditioning, may regress spiritually and will have to regain the lost ground subsequently.

I can't offer proof of reincarnation. I can only repeat that it is a fact. After that it's a question of personal belief. It is well that all souls should be aware of the different possibilities of development, of which reincarnation is one.

Reincarnation and Awareness

Souls will reach their own conclusions about reincarnation as they are ready for them. In any event, conclusions reached through proof don't have nearly as much value from an awareness point of view as conclusions reached through reason or, ideally, through inner knowing.

For anybody who accepts that reincarnation is a fact I would like to elaborate a little. In the early stages of human existence, a life-span was generally much longer than it is now; it averaged about 500 years. As things evolved, with free will expressing itself in many different ways, the grand design kept adjusting itself to accommodate the changing conditions. Because the lifestyles of many led to a diminution of their awareness, the application of effective corrective measures became difficult. The grand designers felt that this could more successfully be done with shorter repeated physical lives by which means they hoped that tendencies established in one would not be too firmly entrenched to be offset in another. From its beginning, Earth was designed as a vehicle by which awareness would be increased, but it was not originally a part of the grand design that there should be repeated human existences on Earth. As with the initial fall from awareness, shorter physical life-spans accompanied by opportunities for reincarnation were a counterbalancing result of the ways in which free will continued to express itself.

Reincarnation, then, represents a stage of evolution in the grand design. The increasing world population is largely a consequence of reincarnation (and also of souls progressing from the first to the second stage). The purpose of reincarnation is to give souls repeated opportunities to raise their awareness. Earth provides a wide range of those opportunities.

What are the criteria for determining whether one has mastered all the lessons of Earth? Essentially these are:

- Acceptance of oneness with all life.
- Being at one with all life.
- Absolute tolerance of others; their opinions, their way of life, how and what they are.
- Total respect for the free will of others.
- Acceptance of the continuity and of the spirituality of life (which implies recognition of spiritual being as distinct from physical being). You are a soul with a body not a body with a soul.
- And most important, total acceptance of one's place in God (a part of God, equal to each other part).

Put like that, they don't seem to be all that much—but they encompass a lot of turmoil, unfortunately. Once a soul has acquired these attributes, Earth has nothing more to offer it unless it chooses to reincarnate to help others.

Reincarnation and Time

You want me to consider two questions:

1. If everything is constantly happening now in an eternal present how can there be such a thing as reincarnation unless each soul is in some way fragmented into different personalities?
2. If the concept of time does not exist in reality, that is, in spirit, why is it a part of the Earth scene?

To take the second question first: Earth was designed as a vehicle for learning experiences. A linear time sequence was a simple aid to learning; one experience would follow another and the lessons of each would be absorbed in an orderly way. Always the primary objective is growth in awareness; the progression of time as you know it is simply a device to help to achieve that objective.

Even on Earth, however, there are clear reflections of a continuing present. Day repeats itself into night and season into season; the Earth keeps on moving round the sun; thus an appearance of change is created so that it can truthfully be said in apparently contradictory terms that everything in nature changes but yet remains the same. If the Earth were to stop moving time would stand still; in other words, Earth and time travel hand in hand.

I refer back to my analogy of Earth as a merry-go-round. You jump on (are born) at one point and jump off (die) at another. You may jump on and off many times during the course of the round.

Now imagine that before you jump on each time you change your appearance in some way so that outwardly you seem to be a different person. At many stages during the round you appear in different guises.

Suppose that a spirit is looking down from above the merry-go-round. He sees you getting on and off in all your different appearances. He sees you creating an illusion of movement without actually going anywhere. He himself is neither taking up space nor moving through time. For him time and space have no meaning; for you the timing of your getting on and off, and the space and appearance you choose each time on the merry-go-round, are most significant.

However, if you see time and space in a different way, as a creative process of mental development and expansion, then the words have meaning within the reality of spirit. Each physical incarnation is intended as a process of development. In the wider meaning of time, therefore, physical existences of one soul cannot be said to take place simultaneously any more than they do in the physical time scale. The passage of time is really a record of progression towards the ultimate objective of full awareness. Physical existence illustrates the progression in a simple way with its framework of time and space, i.e., movement from one point to the next, to the next, and so on in a linear sequence.

Spirit is endlessly creative; so that if you equate time with creativity rather than with movement from day to night, etc., then time is a fact of all life, physical and spirit, and there is no confusion of meaning.

When you are jumping on and off the merry-go-round you change your appearance each time. You shed the outer shell but you do not fragment the real you. As you grow in awareness you also shed the attributes which had previously clouded your awareness, but they are no part of you nor were they ever, although you may have hugged them to you for centuries (e.g., possessiveness, intolerance). Fragmentation of soul was a product of the original fall from awareness; given free will, it can still happen but it is not likely to because of the flexibility of the grand design in adjusting itself to the vagaries of free will. The fully aware soul is an integrated entity and will always remain so. Once a soul reaches the second stage it is also an integrated entity and it is unlikely that the grand design will fail to ensure that it remains so until it reaches full awareness.

One of the hallmarks of creativity is simplicity. Any concept of an entity endlessly fragmenting itself into different personalities is too complex to be creative in any positive sense of the word. I leave you to submit the matter to your own reasoning processes.

Group Reincarnation

Souls tend to reincarnate in groups. The sizes of groups vary; in human terms they are usually quite large, often running into millions. Within the groups there are sub-groups which for many reasons have chosen to operate contrasting interrelationships in different Earth lives. For example, souls may choose to have roles as husbands and wives in contrasting sexual relationships in a number of lifetimes, or they may choose to be brothers or sisters, or parents and children. It all depends on what they want to learn in a lifetime. The souls with whom they choose to interrelate are those who they feel can best help them with their life purpose, and vice versa.

As I have already explained, the reason why souls don't generally remember their previous lives on Earth is in order to allow them to have a fresh start without the burden (of guilt, e.g.) which remembrance would place on them. At the same time the present can be helped by the past. For example, if a person is having problems with a particular relationship it can be helpful to him to know how those problems originated and to realize that part of his life purpose is to overcome the problems by mental adjustment to them within the restrictive Earth setting. Or if a person has an obsessive interest in sex, or gambling, or eating, or alcohol, or anything at all, it can be beneficial to get to the source of the obsession. This is something that cannot be done by traditional methods, such as psychiatry, unless the obsession originated in the present lifetime, which is most unlikely.

The key to helpfulness, in my view, is selectivity in the presentation of experiences, both in the manner of presentation as well as in the experiences themselves. A medium or counselor, psychiatrist or psychotherapist, working under the guidance of evolved souls can best do this. In that way, the person enjoys the possibility of understanding and accepting through knowledge without having to undergo the trauma of remembrance. Also, the evolved souls will make sure that only information which will be of help to him in his present situation will be passed on to him; in other words, idle curiosity will not be satisfied in a purposeless way.

Euthanasia and Suicide

Each soul, in conjunction with its guides, if it decides to have guides, designs its physical existence, including the timing of the birth and death of its body. This raises questions such as, how euthanasia and suicide fit into the design, if they do.

There is one clear distinction between euthanasia and suicide, which is that euthanasia is performed by somebody else whereas suicide is self-operated. Euthanasia may, of course, be performed as a result of an earlier request by the person concerned, but essentially that is suicide.

Euthanasia, in the sense of an act performed, usually with altruistic motivation, by another or others on a person without the consent of that person is an interference with free will and, accordingly, falls into the category of unawareness. For that reason I don't intend to dwell on it any further.

Suicide, in the sense of an act voluntarily performed by a person on himself, is an expression of free will and, accordingly, may fall into either category of awareness or unawareness. Every human being commits suicide in one way or another.

The thrust of traditional teaching in this area is that God creates each soul and each body and that only God has the right to decide the timing and the manner of the birth and death of each body. However, once you accept that each soul is a part of God you can look on the matter from a different viewpoint. Once you further accept that each soul designs its own body and its own life on Earth before it enters into the body, your whole perspective is changed. Now you are the creator. And, of course, it is still true to say that God is the creator in that you are part of God, but obviously it's an inadequate and misleading version of truth once it's expressed without elaboration.

When I say that every human being commits suicide in one way or another, I'm thinking first of the fact that each soul's life plan comprehends the birth and death of the body that it has designed for a projected Earth existence. Second, there's the fact that the plan also comprehends the manner of that birth and death. The plan in one case may envisage death by means of a heart attack; in another through a form of cancer; in another by way of a car crash; in another through an overdose of sleeping pills, and so on. The important thing to bear in mind is that the manner of death of the body is determined in the soul's pre-earth-existence life plan. However, as has been outlined in earlier sessions, the plan is not always adhered to and many of what are commonly termed suicides are more likely to be deviations from than adherence to plan; for example, when they are committed in unbalanced, e.g., depressive, states of mind.

It is a very unwise exercise for any person to pass judgment on another because of that person's manner of death; indeed, to pass judgment for any reason. Each soul's plan is specially designed to cater to its needs, and even if it deviates from it, the grand design will adjust itself to the deviation(s) and eventually all will be well for that soul. So do not grieve for anybody who commits suicide in a more obvious way than others in his community; and, above all, don't waste your energy and, in the process, retard your own development by making, and perhaps acting on, assumptions about his eternal future.

Is it advisable to try to find out what manner of death one has chosen? Usually, no. It is easier for people to fulfill their life purpose if they live in the present. The knowledge of when and how they are going to die would likely be a constraining burden for most people to carry. The lessons of each day have more impact if its experiences are not foreseen. This, after all, is why the grand design provided that people would not remember their plans while on Earth.

Death: What Happens?

In the session on the second stage of evolutionary growth I outlined in a broad way what happens when a soul leaves its physical body. Obviously, the circumstances in which a soul finds itself on transition vary with each individual soul and depend on its state of mind at the time of the death of the body.

Take the case of a man who dies believing that there's nothing beyond the death of the body. He is convinced that he is still alive on Earth and even though he sees his body being buried or cremated he thinks that a horrible mistake has been made. He stays around his relatives and friends trying to get somebody to listen to him. He can't understand why he's not getting through to them. He sees them grieving for him and talking about him as if he were dead. It's a time of much confusion for him.

Meanwhile, souls in spirit, including his guide or guides, if he had agreed to have any for his Earth lifetime, are trying to help him. While he's in a state of confusion and single-minded concentration on trying to get somebody on Earth to listen to him, it is unlikely that the other souls will be able to get through to him. In any event, they will probably feel that he's not yet ready to accept his present state. Since he's no longer bound by time in the same way as on Earth he's not conscious of the passage of time. In Earth terms his confusion may even cover a period of years, but while that sounds bad to somebody on Earth it's not so bad in the spirit sense. The closest analogy I can give is that of a person who suffers a concussion and is not aware of what is going on around him. Yet he continues with what he was doing before the concussion though he will have no recollection of this later, nor will he have any idea of how long he was concussed.

Ultimately the souls who are waiting to help get their opportunity. The most likely way for this to happen is through a soul who was either a relative or a friend of his while on Earth. His concentration on the Earth scene will slacken at some stage and the other soul chooses this opportunity to bring itself to his attention. Once he accepts that he has, in fact, died in the physical sense but that he is still alive in reality and that life is a continuity, he is on the road to adjustment to his new condition. There are many souls available to help him according to his capacity to receive help.

People who have no belief in life after death are in the most difficult condition of all in so far as adjustment to life in spirit is concerned. That's why acceptance of the continuity of life is the most basically advantageous condition for any soul.

The next most difficult condition is where a person has totally inflexible beliefs about life in spirit. For example, if he believes that after death he will be judged by God and consigned to a place of reward or punishment, maybe for eternity or maybe until a final Day of Judgment when his body will be miraculously rejoined with his soul to experience an eternity of heaven or hell, he may well continue to be limited by those beliefs for a long time. He will continue this way until he begins to wonder why things aren't happening the way he expected they would. Or perhaps his association with other souls who may have started to change their beliefs may also bring him to question his beliefs.

The best condition of all in which to make the transition is one of complete acceptance of the continuity of life, of individual responsibility for spiritual development, and of the fact that there are many evolved souls only waiting to be asked for help. A soul leaving its body in that frame of mind will make rapid progress through the stages back to full awareness. The shuttered mind is the most impenetrable barrier of all against spiritual progress.

How can people best help their friends or relatives or acquaintances who have died, or, indeed, the "dead" generally? The best way to help is by asking your guides to convey your concern and love to them and to suggest to them that the guides will provide all the help they need if they are prepared to accept such help. The guides will find the most suitable opportunity to do this.

I can only recommend the way that seems best and simplest to me. Others use different ways, including prayer.

Although they may succeed I personally wouldn't recommend any way other than the one I have outlined. I'll try to explain why.

If, say, a group of individuals pray to God for a particular soul, their thoughts are concentrated on that soul while they are praying and presumably they are asking that it should be granted eternal happiness. It is unlikely that any two of them will have coinciding views as to what constitutes eternal happiness. All those thoughts form a powerful pressure around the soul and because the thoughts are more than likely in conflict with each other (for example, in their conception of eternal happiness) the pressure may be extremely inharmonious, thus causing much confusion in the recipient (or victim!). The prayers may succeed in that the pressure may become so unbearable that the soul has to seek help, but I'm sure it's not the wish of those praying that their prayers should be answered in that way.

Prayer isn't, of course, the only method used by people for trying to help the dead. Groups of people come together and invite earthbound souls to communicate with them so that they can talk to them and advise them. Individuals and groups also use other methods, such as ouija boards or seances or mediumistic communication. All of these methods may be helpful but unless they are guided and controlled by evolved souls they may also be harmful for instance, by giving unaware souls free rein to act mischievously even to the extent, sometimes, of pretending to be relatives or friends of the people attempting communication.

Souls are sometimes referred to as being trapped, e.g., in a belief that they are still alive on Earth, and there is a school of thought that because these souls are earthbound they can only be directly helped by people on Earth. While sometimes it may be convenient for souls in spirit to use humans to help them to help souls who are having difficulty adjusting to changed conditions, and this is probably done as a means of helping the humans also, it isn't necessary for them to do so.

In a sense every soul who has not yet regained full awareness is trapped in its feeling and thinking. However, no soul is ever abandoned; the grand design has seen to that. Help is provided when the time is right without any interference with free will. Nobody can free a trapped soul but itself. When it accepts the help available to it, it is on the road to freedom. Anybody who claims that he frees trapped souls is simply deluding himself and/or others.

Caution in Communicating

As you know, the difficulty with communication between souls temporarily in human form and other souls is that the others can't readily be seen. Because of this humans are at a disadvantage in deciding whether apparent communications are products of their own subconscious or are genuine communications from spirit and, if genuine, whether the interpretation or wording given to them is accurate.

It is part of the grand design that humans should not generally be aware of other souls around them. They are on Earth to benefit from the human experience, which means limiting themselves to the constraints of Earth and in trying to overcome them to learn whatever lessons they need to learn. The ideal thing, in my view, is to be able to combine unobtrusive communication (e.g., with guides) with day-to-day living so that one blends with the other and helps with it.

Some people make communication with "the spirit world" part of their daily living so that it becomes their work.

They will have chosen to do this before coming on Earth and will have specially prepared their bodies in order to facilitate communication. They are commonly called mediums. There are different forms of mediumship, such as trance, or inspirational, or automatic writing. In trance mediumship the human agent seems to be in a trance while a soul or souls in spirit apparently use his voice box. In inspirational mediumship the human agent receives thoughts or impressions from a soul or souls in spirit and puts his own interpretation and words on them. With automatic writing the human agent merely allows his hand to be used and is unconscious of what is being produced.

The first point I want to make is predictable and is one that the reader of the record of these sessions is probably tired of seeing repeated. It is that any person who is involved in mediumship of any kind should make sure to ask his guides to control the flow of communication. Otherwise he is likely to find himself in the business of self-delusion and of deluding others no matter how sincere he may be about what he's trying to do.

It is not possible for any soul to take over the body of another even if the human were willing to allow that to happen. So in trance mediumship the human's body is not taken over by a soul in spirit. What happens is that a form of self-hypnosis takes place. The mediums, for whatever reason, don't have the courage to admit even to themselves that what's really happening is that thoughts are being impressed on their minds and that they are relaying those thoughts. In other words, while they express their willingness to participate in the events by freely donating the use of their bodies, they are at the same time afraid of that participation in some way. So they sidestep their fear by convincing themselves, even to the extent of changing completely their vocal form of expression, that spirit beings are temporarily using their bodies. This doesn't necessarily in any way take from the validity of the communications that they transmit. It's just a fact that there's no difference between trance and inspirational mediumship in so far as the actual method of transmission is concerned. Automatic writing is different in that all that's involved is willingness on the human's part to allow his hand to be moved over a sheet of paper; he can, of course, stop the movement at any time.

Anybody who chooses to be a medium takes on a big responsibility. If he misleads himself or allows himself to be misled he is living a lie which will add to the debt he owes himself as a part of God. Because he has no way of proving whether much of the information he gets is true or false he has no way of avoiding being misled unless he takes the precaution of having his communications controlled by an evolved soul or souls. Having taken that precaution he can then rely absolutely on the validity of the communications he receives from spirit sources. He may still have difficulties of interpretation, but this is part of his own learning experience and should naturally become less and less with experience in direct proportion to the thoroughness with which he learns from experience.

I strongly recommend that all communications that purport to come from spirit whether they come directly or through a medium should be tested for genuineness. This can best be done through guides.

In your own case you want to apply the test to what you have written in these sessions. Since from an early stage in your conscious communication with spirit you asked that your guides should control all further communication, you need have no doubts whatever about the validity or genuineness of what has been transmitted to you. Insofar as these sessions are concerned you have given expression in substance to my thoughts with one-hundred-percent accuracy.

The wording you use is, of course, a matter of your own style; far be it from me to be critical of that!

So I'm glad to be able to confirm to you your feeling that you're being true to yourself, which is all any soul can hope to be. You need have no doubts about sharing with others these sessions. They are honest expressions of our truth (I, of course, include your guides in the "our"). What others take from them is their affair and their responsibility—and their opportunity.

Trance Mediumship: Games

It may be well to devote a little more time and space to the subject of trance mediumship. You are somewhat troubled by an apparent contradiction to the effect that in trance mediumship the human's body is not taken over by a soul in spirit but that a form of self-hypnosis takes place and what you have heard and read about different trance mediums whose method of speaking, and appearance even, are often completely changed and who have no recollection of what transpired during a "performance." The word "performance" is actually a suitable word to use in this context because the medium is, in fact, putting on a show. The medium may be a retiring person or lacking in self-confidence or even somewhat doubtful or skeptical, but yet a person of sincerity and integrity who wishes to be of service to others; the trance method offers a neat solution to the dilemma of how to provide the service.

All human beings are actors. Life on Earth is as much an illusion as life portrayed on a stage. The value of both is in their capacity to raise awareness. A play that is well-written, well-directed, and well-performed will often have more impact than a conversation. People will tend to accept, more readily, information that seems to be more obviously coming from a disembodied spirit than an embodied one. Even though the embodied one may claim to be receiving communication from a spirit source, there is always the possibility for his audience that he is letting his imagination or his own personal views or interpretations take over. Elements of drama are incorporated in a trance performance.

The grand design accommodates an infinite variety of methods of raising awareness. Souls in spirit and in physical bodies cooperate with each other in the implementation of the design. Trance mediumship is one form of expression of such cooperation.

It seems to me that, in general, human beings take themselves far too seriously. Life on Earth is full of challenges, yes, or it wouldn't be of any value as a learning experience; but it was never intended to be a vale of tears. Today's crisis is usually gone by the time tomorrow becomes today. How well do you remember the happenings of last week, not to mention last month or last year? The game doesn't matter; it's how you play whatever game you choose that matters.

We seem to have moved from trance mediumship to playing games. Yet it's not really a move. All happenings are games. The only reality is consciousness. And consciousness in its aware state is joy, happiness, bliss, all included in love. Any game that helps people to realize that more fully is worth playing.

How Best to Deal with Death

It's a fact of life on Earth that people die. Even though it hasn't happened to you yet (in this life), you know that it will. You know that your body will cease to exist. It's the vehicle that enables you to experience life on Earth and when its work is done you (the soul) will leave it and it will be transformed into ashes or dust.

No one who has ever assumed physical form has escaped from the experience of the death and disintegration of the body. That's a categorical statement which cuts across traditional belief systems; for example, the Christian beliefs in the physical assumption into heaven of Jesus and, in the case of some Christians, of Mary, his mother. Since Jesus was proclaimed the only Son of God, the ordinary laws of nature couldn't be seen to apply to him, nor, more arguably, to his mother. He couldn't be born in the same way as ordinary human beings, his mother couldn't go through the human process of conception, nor could they die as ordinary mortals. So myths were created and perpetuated as dogma, and human beings were deprived of the very identification that Jesus wanted them to feel with him in his humanity/divinity.

Even though many people can accept that there's no death, that life on Earth is simply a transitory stage in an evolutionary process designed to lead to growth in awareness, and that there's no such thing as the soul being judged and punished for its transgressions of divine law by an arbitrary God, physical separation is painful. No matter what one's level of awareness is, there's a deep sadness, often a desolation, about looking at the dead body of somebody one has loved, remembering the mannerisms, their way of talking, looking, touching, smiling, laughing, the association of places, a favorite chair, clothes, the grim finality of knowing that there will never again in this lifetime be physical contact with that person. Even when one can feel the continuity of contact in a spiritual way, and many people do and are increasingly allowing themselves to accept it, it's comforting, but it's just not the same as the physical presence.

It's a feature of life on Earth that interpersonal relationships come and go. For example, two people who had a very close relationship with each other as school friends, went their separate ways and, on meeting many years later, find that they have little to say to each other. Romantic relationships blossom, wither, and die. As people move from one work situation to another, friendships with former colleagues are inevitably replaced by friendships in the new situation. The separation in many cases is just as final as physical death, although, of course, that's disguised by the fact that the people parting from each other are still in animate bodies.

People, then, are used to dealing with change and adapting themselves to it. Although many people say they don't like change, if they think about it they will see that they are managing it regularly in unconscious ways. It's such a feature of physical life that everybody has to learn to cope with it in some way; and, of course, change is designed to help growth in awareness.

In so far as death is concerned, it's still change, but the severity of its impact lies in the fact that it presents itself in such a final way. Accordingly, people can't adapt to it as easily as they do to other changes. I know that some changes such as marriage breakdowns can have traumatic and long-lasting effects, but there's still a possibility of physical contact, which death doesn't offer.

How can you best deal with death? I'd like to offer the following suggestions:

- Don't try to be superhuman; allow yourself to grieve;
- Bear in mind that each human being is really a soul with a body and that life on Earth was deliberately designed for growth purposes as a temporary state of being;
- Don't shut yourself off from the person who has died; that soul will still want to keep in contact with you and, as long

as neither of you is in a continuing depressed state, the contact will be mutually rewarding;

* When you get a feeling of contact, don't argue yourself out of it (always a logical thing to do);
* In the early stages of the separation set aside a little time each day to talk to the one who has died. Don't worry if you feel a little foolish doing that; I can assure you that the soul will hear you (there's no communication more powerful than a link of love);
* Send love regularly to the soul.

The above are some ways that I hope you will find helpful in dealing with the physical separation of death, getting on with your own life, and preparing for your own death.

With the acceleration of growth in consciousness at present happening on Earth, fear of what is called the supernatural is diminishing and more people are open to the possibility of communication between souls in different dimensions. What is seen as exceptional today, or "off the wall," will become commonplace within the lifetimes of many people now on Earth. As a result, separation through physical death will become much less painful than it is at present.

In case of misunderstanding, I should say that my suggestions are intended primarily for those who wish to preserve contact with people whose bodies have died; in other words, where there's a mutually loving bond, not a controlling one.

Further Elaboration on the First Stage

The difference between the first and second stages is that the soul has not reached a high enough level of awareness to enable it, in the opinion of the grand designers, to operate as an integrated entity with free will. Thus at the first stage one soul may be housed simultaneously in a multiplicity of bodies, e.g., insects, but this doesn't happen at the second stage; a soul uses only one human body at a time.

I have chosen to discuss this again because, while you take my word for it, you nevertheless find it a daunting and somewhat ridiculous idea that all sorts of fish and birds and animals and creepy crawly things are, in fact, souls. What idea would you find more acceptable? That all these creatures exist for no reason other than as a fact of nature? That they are there for the sustenance and use of humans? That they serve a mysterious divine purpose and that is all you need to know about them?

There is no proof I can now give you or anybody on Earth that what I say is so is, in fact, so. All I can do is hope that my outline will prove acceptable to reason supported by observation of the orderly pattern of nature and non-human life on Earth.

The strongest instinct in all living beings is that of survival. Some souls became so fragmented and reached such a low level of awareness that they became almost totally unconscious (or subconscious) of themselves and of others, somewhat like a person in a coma. The grand designers needed some ingredient that would rouse those souls from the apathy that seemed to have become their permanent condition. The creation of physical life in multiple, specially-designed forms, and the installation in those forms of brains with an overriding instinct for survival supplied that ingredient. In the spiritual sense, survival is an unreal concept since non-survival is an impossibility. In the limited physical sense the implantation of an idea of survival, spread through a multiplicity of brains, is sufficient to bring about a consciousness of life and helps to encourage souls to continue the journey back to full awareness.

Evolved souls watch over all aspects of the grand design. It is difficult to conceive of a soul being temporarily fragmented into, say, a million fleas. Don't think of it as a physical concept; think of it rather as an attempt to spread consciousness. The physical vehicles are specially chosen by the evolved soul or guide who has responsibility for that particular soul, and the growth in the soul's level of consciousness is carefully monitored. At the insect stage survival is of paramount importance. At later stages the soul has more scope for self-development for instance, in giving and receiving love.

I have already given my views on the eating of meat to the effect that if it is done with respect, it is not a barrier to, and may help, growth in awareness. The grand design comprehends the killing and eating of one form of physical non-human being by another. While in physical terms this may seem to be barbaric, it, in fact, strengthens the instinct for survival in both the killer and the killed. As the instinct for survival is sublimated or supplemented by development of other feelings, the soul becomes more and more integrated so that at the second stage it is no longer fragmented. It is usually unthinkable for human beings that they should physically eat each other. It would, of course, be likely to be an interference with free will that this should happen. As free will is not operative at the first stage, the killing and eating of non-human beings by human beings is not an interference with free will. However, if the killing is accomplished with cruelty, or is, for example, regarded as a sport, the awareness of the perpetrators may be adversely affected.

Is it a help towards increasing awareness to be vegetarian? It doesn't matter. In order to survive on Earth it is necessary for a person to eat. What he eats comes from living physical substance and it is only the physical substance that's consumed. A soul cannot be eaten!

Many people are cruel to animals because they don't understand that they are also souls. Cruelty is often described as mindless; I can't think of a more apt description, given that mind is soul. Cruelty is a negation of soul to the extent that it obscures the loving nature of soul. I include all forms of cruelty, both physical and mental, although, of course, all cruelty is, in fact, mental. There are obvious forms of cruelty such as torture, or what are known as blood sports, but there are many less obvious ones, such as abandonment or neglect of dependent creatures; cruelty may often result from nothing more negative than mere thoughtlessness. Whatever about its manifestations or apparent consequences, the perpetrator of cruelty ultimately causes most damage to himself, to his own awareness. Neither the hare which is pursued and mangled by dogs nor the dogs who do the pursuing and mangling are likely to be damaged in any way near the same extent as the organizers and participants in the event.

But what about animals which are commonly considered to be a source of infection or disease or, at least, uncleanness, such as rats, or mice, or flies? Is it cruel to kill them? It's not possible to give a yes or no answer. It depends on the circumstances. In general, I think it best for a person's awareness that he should, as far as possible, avoid all forms of violence and treat all life with respect.

Many concerned people and many not so concerned people put animals down for one reason or another. Again, this is something that is best avoided, in my opinion. Animals are also working out their own life purpose, with guidance, under the grand design. They know instinctively when their time is up and they arrange their own going if they are allowed to do so. It is difficult for a person to watch his beloved pet suffering, but that may be a valuable experience for both of them. From the spiritual point of views what's important is not what happens to the physical body but the effect that that happening produces on the mind.

Now you're worried about what you think is an apparent contradiction between my saying that the killing and eating of animals, if done with respect, is consistent with growth in spirituality, whereas the putting down of animals, even when done out of love and consideration for them, is not. Ideally, life on Earth, including physical survival, is all one big cooperative effort designed to raise awareness all round. An animal whose physical body is killed and eaten is helping in that cooperative effort in the most basic way by contributing towards the physical survival of another or others. This cannot be said in the case of an animal that is put down. A person who takes an animal into his care becomes a partner with the evolved soul who has taken on responsibility for the soul which is temporarily and partly manifested physically in that animal. The animal's life is precious and its duration has been determined under the umbrella of the grand design by its guide. Remember, free will is not yet operative in its case.

I don't want to say to anybody, in fact, it is not open to me to say to anybody, "This is what you must do," or, "this is what you mustn't do." But, if I am to provide the most helpful information, I have to say that, in general, termination of physical life other than for survival purposes is not likely to be in accordance with the grand design.

But is it not an expression of deep love towards a distressed, terminally ill animal to have it put down to save it suffering? It may seem to be, but, in reality (that is, spiritually) it is a lack of awareness. Ask yourself, would you have a child put down in the same situation? If not, why not? The child is in your care also, is incapable of exercising free will as yet, and apparently doesn't understand its suffering any more than the animal. If you accept that they are both souls, the parallel is exact.

Finally, how about the use of animals for experimental or research purposes in the interests of furthering scientific or medical knowledge? I think that the best way I can answer that question is by asking another, how would you feel about a child being used in that way?

Animals and Death

What happens to animals when they die? As we have seen, what appears in physical form as an animal incorporates only part of a soul (or mind). The first goal is the reunion of all the parts into one individual soul. The second and ultimate goal is the regaining of full awareness by the soul.

It may be helpful if we take an example of, say, a dog that becomes ill and dies. Its guide helps it through the transition in such a way that it is not, in fact, aware of the transition for some time, the equivalent of a day or so in your time. This period of rest (like sleep) is necessary so that the mental effects of the illness will be overcome. When it becomes conscious, it is still in the etheric equivalent of its physical body but without infirmity of any kind. The first sensation it feels is hunger and immediately a dish of its favorite food appears before it. The thought of the food produces it; the power of thought to actualize itself is much more obvious in spirit than it is on Earth. The power itself is not less on Earth; its effects are less obvious. Food is not necessary for survival in spirit and, of course, its substance is not material; but neither is the substance of the etheric body. What is produced as food can be just as real and as palatable to the etheric body as material food is to the physical body.

When its hunger is satisfied, the dog's next thought is of its people, who are themselves also thinking of it and grieving over its passing. No sooner thought than done; the dog is immediately with them. They can feel its presence if they don't reason themselves out of the feeling or if they are aware enough to recognize it. It is possible for its guide to communicate with the dog in such a way that it realizes that its people cannot see it and therefore cannot show their love for it in the same way as they did while it was in its physical body; but that they still love it as much as ever.

It's a feature of life on Earth that it's full of partings, in a physical sense, of one kind or another, the most notable being the death of the physical body. It's a great comfort to people if they can accept that these partings are not real; one soul is never more than a thought away from another.

To return to the dog; it stays with its people, or comes and goes to them, as long as both sides need the contact. At the same time it is being reintroduced to its other soul part which had already completed a physical existence, also as a dog. According as souls progress through various forms of animal life, fragmentation decreases until at the level of domestic animals it is likely to be limited to two or three simultaneous or nearly simultaneous physical manifestations. One of the characteristics of domestic animals, which you may have noticed, is that they don't see themselves as being any different from human beings. Their awareness is sharpened by their contact with humans even to the extent of gauging the humans' often variable moods and accepting their behavioral inconsistencies.

In any event, their guides place the two dogs in contact with each other for long periods. They become more and more attuned to each other's thought processes. They are being guided towards a merging of awareness or consciousness so that eventually they will become one integrated soul or mind. At that stage the reintegrated soul is ready to reassume the privilege (or burden!) of free will and to incarnate as a human being if it so wishes.

The same process happens in varying degrees with all other forms of animal life. When they pass on from their Earth existence they are continually guided towards a merging of consciousness. The transition is slow; breaking down mental barriers always is. But it is a steady movement with all the patience and wisdom and support and love of a myriad of evolved souls behind it.

Learning from Animals

In earlier sessions, we discussed how the grand design operates through different stages of growth, with consciousness spreading through non-human life, which is how animals fit into the evolutionary process until they achieve the capacity to exercise free will in human form.

During this session I'm confining our consideration to domestic animals, specifically, dogs and cats, and their relationship with human beings. I have chosen dogs and cats particularly because they are preparing to move more immediately into the human state.

Ideally, dogs and cats live with people and learn from them how to be lovingly human. People, in turn, again ideally, learn from their pets how to make progress on their human journey.

Of course, dogs and cats can't be lumped together, any more than humans can; they have their own characteristics, both as species and individually. I'm only generalizing about them for illustrative purposes.

If one accepts that all life is comprehended by the grand design, it's extremely important that all animals should be treated with respect and love.

When you love a dog or a cat there will be shades of difference in how they respond to you; a cat may, initially at least, seem to be more detached than a dog. But of one thing you can be sure, you will see beyond all doubt how love given freely is returned and multiplied. People can learn from dogs—yes, and cats, too—how to love unconditionally.

Why is it, then, that, if dogs and cats can love unconditionally so readily, the stages of evolution don't go the other way; in other words, that human beings progress towards becoming dogs and cats? The big difference is, of course, that dogs and cats aren't aware of themselves in the same way as humans are. They act in feeling ways, but the feeling is limited by its lack of awareness of itself; in ultimate expression, feelings and thoughts are balanced in loving awareness. When a soul is ready to move from the animal to the human state it has reached a level of consciousness where it will be able to incorporate thinking into its feeling. You'll notice how this works with a child. Initially, a child is very like a dog or a cat in that it responds to life in a totally feeling way; it isn't yet aware of itself as a human being.

A major difficulty for a human as he moves from childhood to adolescence and adulthood is that his conditioning is likely to create an imbalance between his feelings and thoughts; usually, he's controlled by his patterns of thought, which are conditioned by environmental, etc., influences. In observing a dog or a cat, in communicating with it, above all, in loving it, he will be helped to achieve a balance. He will not be able to mask his feelings from a dog or a cat in the same way as he may be with a fellow human. In releasing his feelings for the animal he is helping himself to release them more truly towards people.

Part VI

Dialogue with Shebaka

Paddy: I accept and, indeed, I know that there are at present all sorts of global evidences of growth in awareness in a general way. But at the same time there seems to be a lot of unrestrained violence. For example, some people appear to have no qualms about torturing and killing helpless elderly men and women; not to mention, of course, the mass horrors that are all too often perpetrated in different parts of the world. Do you still feel optimistic about the planet?

Shebaka: Yes. Violence in all its forms, is an expression of inner conflict. When all people find peace in themselves there will be no violence. I'm optimistic because I can see how many people are looking, and are beginning to look, within themselves. All through the evolution of the planet, people have been looking to gods and gurus of one kind or another to tell them what to do. Now more and more people are accepting that the divine is within each of them and as they let it manifest they love themselves and each other unconditionally. Of course, it's a gradual process, and the conflict in change can be intense. Freedom, once surrendered, is not easily regained. But the tide of divine love, as people are now allowing it to express itself in them, is flowing too strongly to be turned back.

Paddy: I know that in the utopian scheme of things there won't be any crime and, therefore, no need for penal systems.

In the meantime society is burdened with hugely expensive systems of law enforcement, often culminating in locking people up for varying periods of time with little or no rehabilitative effects; in fact, the reverse in many cases. Have you any comments or suggestions?

Shebaka: I'm sure there would be general agreement that the ideal situation would be one where all people are at peace with one another with total respect for each individual's "space." Obviously, that means that there would be no violation of anybody's person or territory. It would follow that there would be no need for the present panoplies of law enforcement arrangements.

Even looked at purely from an economic point of view that sounds eminently sensible, doesn't it? And if it is true that the vast majority of people want it, why isn't it happening?

The simple answer is that most people are not yet at peace within themselves, although as I have said earlier, I'm optimistic about the rate of progress in that direction, and this is reflected outwardly in conditions around them. That's why I have been concentrating so much in our sessions on the need for each individual to look within first and to find the liberation of taking responsibility for himself. Any community is a reflection of the individuals who comprise it. The more each individual finds fulfillment, the more the community will benefit.

A central question, then, is how can things be orchestrated in such a way that all people individually will have opportunities to expand their awareness and release their divinity within their humanness? That means putting interim arrangements in place as a prelude to the utopian situation.

In general, people who are sentenced to terms of imprisonment feel themselves marginalized in one way or another by the society in which they live. It's true that they chose to be born into society for their own individual reasons. So, ought we take the view that, since that's their choice, it would be an interference with their purpose to attempt to ameliorate their present condition? If we follow that line we're taking a very rigid stance, applying a literal interpretation to the maxim "as you sow so shall you reap" which would mean that no helping hand could ever be given to anybody; for instance, there would be no point at all in having guides/guardian angels.

Everybody on Earth is ultimately aiming to get off the roundabout of cause and effect; clearly that's still an unconscious aim for most of the planet's population. If the systems under which people exist can be changed in order to provide more opportunities for them to find creative fulfillment, that's automatically going to help raise awareness. So now we'll take a look at how the systems can be changed.

We're starting from the base that there would be no crime if all people were at peace within themselves. Releasing creative potential would have the effect of helping people to achieve inner peace. Our challenge, then, is to suggest ways and means by which existing administrative arrangements can facilitate the release of creative potential within everybody without exception.

The scale of the challenge is obvious when we take into consideration the diversity of human existence. Not only are there all differing age levels, but there are also vast gaps in social and material circumstances as well as individual inclinations and capabilities.

I don't want to denigrate the various social and political reforms that have been implemented throughout human history. That they have, to date, been unsuccessful can hardly be denied, but they have been part of an evolutionary process which has brought people to a greater awareness than ever before of how what affects one affects all.

Where do we start? Where else but at the beginning of human life; with children?

It's vitally important that children should be loved and encouraged to express themselves freely. Educational systems should be organized in ways which would facilitate exploration and expression of each child's creative abilities. This would necessarily mean that there would be no set curricula; or, put another way, that there would be an unlimited range of curricula. Each child would get individual attention to a much greater extent than is possible at present. Additional resources would have to be concentrated in education, in its expanded meaning of "drawing forth," but the additional expenditure involved would be more than offset by the resultant elimination of the need for negative punitive measures.

As you know, the reason why the grand design provided that people would be born as children was so that they would be able to make fresh starts. Every child is vulnerable and lovable, and deserves to be loved. No matter what their past life influences may be, children are not born as criminals. Those who later get involved in what are regarded as criminal activities do so as a result of environmental influences and their own reaction to them.

Your question referred particularly to prisons. In my view, prisons are like sores or boils on the face of humanity; they are a negative rather than a positive concentration of energies.

Paddy: A big difficulty is that there are such high levels of unemployment.

Shebaka: The energies of the planet are being used unproductively in many ways. There are more than adequate resources available to provide fulfilling employment for all those who wish to be employed if those resources were to be used in positive rather than negative ways. For example, the purpose of prisons is to lock up people who have been tried and found guilty of having seriously transgressed society's laws. Both the prisoners themselves and the custodial staff are bound together in an enclosed cocoon of energy which is damaging for all of them. If all prisoners, or even a majority of them, find a prison term helpful in increasing their spiritual awareness, prisons might be said to serve a useful purpose. Unfortunately, the opposite is more often the case; a prison term offers opportunities for advanced training in the practical application of criminology!

Paddy: Other options are tried, such as open style institutions for those convicted of what are regarded as less serious offenses, or applying probationary and/or community service formulas under supervision; but society, in its majority opinion, demands for its own protection that those who are found guilty of crimes classified as serious should be locked away so that they are at least out of circulation for some time.

Shebaka: Complexities always arise from trying to deal with symptoms rather than causes. That's true in all areas of life; look, for example, at the medical field. Governments, or those charged with administering a nation/state's affairs, are then always responding to given situations in ways which are designed to bring immediately expedient results. They are continually dealing with one crisis after another. Things don't have to be sorted out all at once. There are many brave pioneering spirits in human form who have already done, and are continuing to do, important work in reforming your educational, etc., systems; and their efforts are drawing attention to the benefits which flow from tackling causes rather than trying to cope with symptom after symptom and getting nowhere.

Paddy: A conveyor belt type organization seemed to be an efficient and logical use of resources in that a person needed to have expertise in one area only. I understand that the impetus for that sort of development came by way of assembly line production of cars. Now, of course, specialization figures largely in all sorts of areas; medicine, law, etc. The rational side of us as human beings likes to break everything into its component parts, so it is an understandable perception that each part could be most effectively dealt with by specialists. Somewhere along the line, though, I think that the human or, I suppose, really the soul factor has been missed. Even though we may often allow ourselves to be treated like robots, deep down we don't like it.

Shebaka: Each soul, whether on its human journey or in spirit, will always have its own particular areas of interest, so that there will eternally tend to be specialization of some kind. Ultimately, for the soul who has regained full awareness, it's rather like specialization within generalization, in other words, each soul has immediate access to whatever there is because it has the ability to link in at all times with the totality of consciousness, but chooses to express itself according to its present inclination. That awareness and freedom are not yet available to those experiencing humanity.

Paddy: Given the compartmentalization that is the trend here on Earth at present, are we stuck with, for instance, our prison systems as they are?

Shebaka: It would be impractical for me to suggest something as radical as the closing down of all prisons immediately, although that's what I would do. People would probably be inclined to regard me as being too much under the influence of spirit(s) to be taken seriously! Physical reality evolves in stages. The foundation has to be the nurturing of children . . . all children. Everything will flow from that.

Paddy: What would you do with a man who abducts a woman, rapes, and kills her in cold blood? I'm assuming that there's no doubt that he's the perpetrator. Our ways of dealing with him would be preventative and punitive to stop him from committing a similar offense and to punish him, either by executing him or locking him up.

Shebaka: That way has also followed through into the perception of how the "sinner" is dealt with after he dies; punishment for all eternity. The human system mirrors a perception of the spirit system, a perception rather than the reality of how it is.

The victim in this case is the woman. Her time on Earth has been arbitrarily cut short, and that can't be changed. No action taken by the state or by anybody else against the man who killed her can restore that particular physical lifetime. So whatever action is taken by the state, apart from its punitive connotations, can only be expressed to be for the common good, a protection for other potential victims, and as a deterrent against any further such acts by the man himself or by others. Whether the man is executed or imprisoned does not affect the karmic debt he owes to the woman he abused and killed. Sooner or later he will have to discharge that debt and no institution and no other person can do that for him.

The notion of punishment to fit the crime doesn't help at all in spiritual terms. Spiritually, there is only self-punishment; indeed, use of the word "punishment" at all is misleading because what happens is a process of self-exploration leading to growth in awareness, which may involve making retribution in some way in respect to acts of violence or cruelty. For example, the man whom we're discussing will, inevitably, given his divine nature, at some future time face what he has done and make compensation to the victim of his violence, not necessarily by an exact reversal of circumstances (which wouldn't be doing her any favors), but by helping her in some appropriate way in her self-realization. The spiritual way is always simple. One is ineluctably faced with oneself and the mirror of one's expression offers no escape from the consequences of that expression; yet, mercifully, there is infinite flexibility in how one can deal with the consequences.

What we're trying to do in our explorations is to reflect as far as possible the way of spirit into the physical world. So, to answer your question, I need to explore how far the spiritual way can be applied to your existing physical circumstances.

Spiritually there's never any question of compulsion. No matter how long it takes, each soul, because its free will is sacrosanct, designs its own journey back to awareness with as much help as it is willing to receive. So, if the man who is the subject of your hypothetical question is arrested, convicted, and sentenced to imprisonment for a number of years, he is not a willing participant in those procedures and is being compelled to comply with them by the state rather than by his own choice. The state assumes the role which much of your religious tradition ascribes to God in eternal terms, although the state is more merciful in that the time scale of the punishment is usually limited!

Paddy: If we leave compulsion out of the reckoning, what's left? Does that mean that the man continues on his merry way, free, maybe, to commit similar acts of violence against others? And, if so, wouldn't others be encouraged to follow his example without any fear of repercussions?

Shebaka: As I have already said, the man will, sooner or later, be his own judge, as will all others be their own judges, including those who may allow themselves to be influenced by his example. But I understand that your question applies to the limited context of the physical framework and, taken on that basis, there must be some response to the man's actions by the state which is representing not alone his immediate victim but all other potential victims.

Paddy: But how can the state make an effective response or, indeed, any response at all without compulsion being involved?

Shebaka: If the state's response is to put the man in prison and/or execute him, it is committing an act of violence against him, however justifiable that act may seem to be in the light of the common good. Therefore, prisons or capital punishment cannot be an ingredient in my answer. At the same time, the man's action cannot be ignored. I suggest that the ideal spiritual response would be to publish, widely, details of what happened as well as a profile of the man himself. That would not be an interference with his free will but would focus attention on him in a way that would encourage him to take responsibility for his actions rather than the state attempting to do so, which is what happens at present.

Paddy: What's to stop him moving from place to place and finding anonymity in that way?

Shebaka: Nothing, but your state systems provide the means to identify him wherever he goes.

Paddy: But that would mean that he could be ostracized all his life, which would be a more severe punishment than being confined in prison for a certain number of years.

Shebaka: It wouldn't be intended as punishment at all but rather as a discharge of the function of government as the agency democratically established by the people to administer the affairs of the state to keep the people informed of whatever might be likely to affect them positively or negatively. How people would respond to the man would be up to each individual, and would potentially be as varied as that. The man might perceive it as punishment, of course, but that would be his choice.

You see, if I may use the parallel of the spirit state, the nonphysical soul is in a vibration where everything is revealed. Suppose, for example, everybody in the physical world was able to see, immediately and completely, everyone else's aura. Then nothing would be hidden. The aura would reveal information about people individually which they would often wish to conceal. So, in order to even things up, as it were, and to apply spiritual considerations to the physical state, the nearest answer, in my view, is to reveal information along the lines we have discussed where somebody has obviously and forcefully invaded another's privacy.

Paddy: I took an extreme example of somebody who commits rape and murder. There are the muggers, the burglars, the so-called petty criminals; and there are those who perpetrate acts of mass violence, such as planting bombs, supposedly for political ends. How can they be allowed to ride roughshod over the wishes, privacy, and physical safety of others? They feel marginalized already; won't they feel even more so if they're branded publicly and identifiably as criminals?

Shebaka: Okay, you're on your own, sitting at home, reading a book or looking at television; just doing whatever you feel like doing and enjoying your own company. Your doorbell rings. You answer it. Two men knock you down and kick you senseless. When you recover consciousness and are able to move, albeit painfully, around the house, you find that many of your valued possessions are gone.

Those men abused you, violated your "space," and stole your property. You may well have to endure long term effects from your injuries. Understandably, you are likely to be feeling angry, shocked, afraid, distressed—any number of mixed emotions.

Whatever develops, the physical damage that has been inflicted on you will not be undone. Your injuries will probably eventually heal; if the contents of your home were insured you may be able to replace some or all of the stolen property, and with the passage of time you may be able to relax and enjoy the comfort of your home again.

As soon as you can, you report the burglary to your local police. As a result of their investigations they establish the identities of the burglars.

It may give you some emotional satisfaction if the two men are put in prison, but clearly that's not going to be of any real benefit to you. You may say that it will stop them temporarily from doing the same thing to another or others, which will please you. However, from a spiritual point of view, the difficulty is that, by depriving the men of their liberty, the state, on your behalf and on behalf of the common good, is invading the men's space, as they invaded yours.

The spiritual principle never changes. Free will is always sacrosanct and not subject to interference or control. I acknowledge that adherence to that principle seems very difficult, if not impossible, in your physical circumstances.

My answer in this case is still the same; publish the details with the identities and descriptions of the burglars.

Paddy: Isn't that invading their privacy?

Shebaka: They created a public profile for themselves by their action; in other words, they surrendered their own privacy. It is up to themselves whether they want to maintain a public profile or not.

Paddy: How effective would publicity of a personal kind be against bombers on the assumption that their identities could be established?

Shebaka: I might turn the question back to you and ask you how effective is imprisonment? I think you will agree that, historically, the answer is, not at all. Draconian measures ultimately always fail. Sometimes they may seem to have a deterrent effect in the short term, but that's all. Invariably they are counterproductive in that they have an inverse inspirational effect. Concentration on negativity reinforces it; so you have an endless cycle of violence seeking to counteract violence.

I understand that what you're doing is playing "devil's advocate" and postulating obvious examples where innocent victims of violence may be left without physical protection. What's basically needed is to create a climate where all people can coexist in peace. That cannot be done as long as punitive practices are in operation. Whether they are state or individually administered is irrelevant.

Paddy: I think I'm safe in concluding that you're not in favor of imprisonment—not to mention capital punishment!

Shebaka: You'll hardly be punished for jumping to conclusions!

Paddy: I'm still concerned, though, about your suggested solution even though I accept that it's an interim one until more radical systems of education are implemented. I'm leaving aside for the moment doubts about the potential effectiveness, or otherwise, of your solution and wondering about the isolationism that seems to be inherent in it. For example, if I commit a burglary and the details are publicized, including my identity, isn't that like putting a stamp or brand on me that I'll be burdened with wherever I go? Wouldn't that be likely to create in me a grudge against society? Once I'm branded, mightn't I as well continue to burgle? Even if I'm very sorry and decide that I never want to do anything like that again, how will I ever free myself from the brand?

Shebaka: Your act of committing a burglary creates the isolation. In doing it you will have separated yourself from your own divinity, which is *the* isolation. If I, as a spirit (non-physical) being, attempt to intrude on others without their consent, or to control them in any way, I automatically exclude myself from an intimacy of communication with them; in other words, I will have separated myself in consciousness from them; if you like, I will have branded myself. Then I will have put myself into a position of having to regain the awareness I lost. I can only do that myself, although I can avail myself of all the help I'm willing to receive.

In my situation, the consequences of my action would be immediately apparent, like a blot on my aura, if I may use an analogy which would make sense to you. However, where you are concerned, because of the density of the physical vibration, the effect on your aura would not be obvious. That's why, if we are endeavoring to synthesize the spirit and physical vibrations, people need to be alerted to the fact that you are a potential intruder on their space.

An immediate and effective way for you to free yourself from the brand would be to make restitution in some form to those whom you have robbed. That action would then also be publicized. If you're not willing to make restitution, which needn't necessarily be of a financial nature, you're not ready to let the brand go.

Paddy: If I commit murder, though, I can't make restitution. I can't restore physical life to the victim.

Shebaka: You could convey your sorrow to the victim through your guides, or even just through your thoughts, and you could offer to perform some appropriate service(s) for the victim's family. How acceptable all that would be to the victim or the victim's family would be a matter for them; in any event, your offer would be a public apology.

Paddy: Under our present systems crimes are investigated by police and courts with the aim of establishing guilt or innocence without doubt. How would you compensate for that?

Shebaka: As I have said, ideally there's always a gradualism about change on Earth. The first priority is education. That will automatically lessen the incidence of crime. I would next begin to phase out the penal institutions. This would be an inevitable progression once the focus of communities would be lovingly rather than fearfully oriented.

Paddy: But suppose somebody is falsely accused and found guilty. A serious injustice would be done to him by his being publicly stigmatized as a criminal.

Shebaka: Yes, but at least he would be more free to get on with his life and perhaps to prove his innocence than if he were shut away in prison.

I would wish that circumstances would never arise where it would be necessary to draw attention to anybody in a way such as I have postulated. That's an unrealistic hope at this stage, unfortunately.

Paddy: I can see how what you're suggesting would work in spirit where you're not concerned with material issues, such as money, or property, and you don't have to cope with the effects of physical injuries; but here on Earth where people are looking for visible forms of preventative measures, such as police, courts, and prisons, your ideas would be likely to be dismissed by many people as being quixotic.

Shebaka: I know. But ask yourself; has experience shown that burglaries, rapes, murders, etc., have been eliminated or even lessened because of perceived deterrent effects of all your law enforcement agencies? All the calls for more laws, more police, more prison places, are reinforcing a climate of fear which feeds violence in one form or another. Radical change is needed, with the central spotlight on education and the fulfillment of creative potential. Fortunately, and designedly, there are many people now on Earth who are attuned to that consciousness. That's why I'm optimistic.

Transformation

Eight butterflies
Spreading gentle wings as a carpet
Across the ghostly path
Of memory.
Caterpillars once,
Carrying within themselves the radiance
Of profligate beauty
Fluttering along the stream
Of awakening consciousness.
A past
Painful in its crawling conditioning
Of seeping shame
Undermining the wonder
Of a fairyland
Rivered on the edge of nowhere;
Yet seeded by its mystic power into
A present
Glorious in its vision
Of being; forever free,
Coming out from under the leaves
Of its self-imposed prison
And revealing itself
For what it is.
The earthbound unlovely caterpillar
Becomes the gorgeous ungravitied butterfly.
The transformation is beyond effort.